Franklin P. Rice, State of Massachusetts, Court of General Sessions of
the Peace

Records of the Court of General Sessions of the Peace

for the County of Worcester, Massachusetts, from 1731 to 1737

Franklin P. Rice, State of Massachusetts, Court of General Sessions of the Peace

Records of the Court of General Sessions of the Peace
for the County of Worcester, Massachusetts, from 1731 to 1737

ISBN/EAN: 9783337221089

Printed in Europe, USA, Canada, Australia, Japan

Cover: Foto ©Suzi / pixelio.de

More available books at **www.hansebooks.com**

RECORDS

OF THE

Court of General Sessions

OF THE PEACE

For the County of Worcester, Massachusetts,

From 1731 to 1737.

Edited by

FRANKLIN P. RICE.

WORCESTER, MASS. :

THE WORCESTER SOCIETY OF ANTIQUITY.

1882.

U. S. A. CVI.

Preface.

THIS VOLUME contains the Records of the Court of General Sessions of the Peace for Worcester County, from August, 1731, to the close of the May term, 1737. The Records of this Court and those of the Inferior Court of Common Pleas for the corresponding period, were entered in the same volume, but were afterwards kept in separate books. The matter here printed forms an important and interesting part of the early history of the County ; and illustrates in a degree the manners and morals of the people of that time. A brief introduction and some notes have been added ; and a full index will be found at the end.

Thanks are due William T. Harlow, Esq. and others in the office of the Clerk of the Courts, for information given, and for facilities afforded in procuring the copy for this volume.

F. P. R.

Introduction.

INTRODUCTION.

IN presenting the Records of the Court of General Sessions of the Peace for the County of Worcester, for the first six years of its existence, a brief review of the origin and growth of the judicial system in Massachusetts will not be out of place. Under the Charter of the Colony, the power of enacting and enforcing laws for the government of its inhabitants was assumed by the Governor, Deputy Governor, Assistants, and the General Court which comprised all the freemen. The General Court met four times a year for the consideration of matters relating to the general government or individual welfare of the community. A monthly court was also held by the Governor, or in his absence, the Deputy Governor, and at least seven Assistants, for the purpose of transacting minor civil or criminal business that required immediate attention. This was termed the Court of Assistants. The Assistants numbered eighteen, and were *ex officio* Justices of the Peace. They discharged the functions of a Council to the Governor.

In 1634 the number of freemen had greatly increased, and some of them having removed to a distance, their meetings became inconvenient and difficult, and delegates were chosen to attend to the affairs of the several towns and districts. This was the origin of the present representative system.

Juries were first established in 1634.[1] In 1639 a law was passed requiring records of the judgments of the courts and magistrates to be kept.[2]

It was not until several years after the establishment of the Colony that a regular system of Courts of Justice was settled, and even then, the powers and jurisdiction of some of them were left vague and indefinite. The principal of these were the General Court, the Court of Assistants, County Courts, Strangers' Courts, Inferior or Magistrates' Courts, Military Courts, and Courts of Chancery.[3] Of these the General Court was supreme, the next in dignity being the Court of Assistants. Appeals lay to them from the inferior courts, and capital offences were tried before the Assistants.

The County Courts, which were established in 1639, had jurisdiction in all cases civil and criminal, except cases of divorce and crimes the penalty whereof extended to life, limb or banishment. They

---

[1] Massachusetts Records, I., 118.　[2] Massachusetts Records, I., 275.
[3] Washburn's Judicial History of Massachusetts.

were presided over by one or more of the Assistants belonging to the county in which the court was held. These courts were authorized to summon grand and petit jurors, and to appoint their own clerks and other officers. Among other duties they laid out highways, licensed houses of entertainment, and were "charged to see that there was an able ministry and that it was well supported."[1] Their functions corresponded nearly with those of the Court of General Sessions established later. They also constituted the Courts of Probate.

No further change of consequence in management or forms was made under the Colonial Government. After the accession of William and Mary and the reception of the Provincial Charter, an act was passed[2] re-organizing the courts under a system which was continued with few modifications until the Revolution. The courts then constituted were, in the order of their importance, Courts of Justices of the Peace, Courts of Quarter Sessions of the Peace, Courts of Common Pleas, a Superior Court, and a Court of Chancery. By an act passed in 1699 the name of the Courts of Quarter Sessions was changed to that of Courts of GENERAL SESSIONS OF THE PEACE.

The jurisdiction of the Courts of General Sessions was partly criminal and partly civil. They could

---

[1] Washburn. Felt's Annals of Salem.   [2] November 25, 1692.

2

hear and determine all matters relating to the conservation of the peace, and the punishment of of-
fenders; and trials were had by juries.   In their
civil capacity they had charge of the financial con-
cerns of their respective counties, controlled the
houses of correction, granted licenses to innholders
and retailers, and located and established highways,
discharging the duties now performed by county
commissioners.   In short these courts had charge
of the prudential affairs of the several counties; and
a general jurisdiction in all criminal matters, the
punishment of which did not extend to life, member
or banishment.[1]   They were presided over by all of
the Justices of the Peace for the county, with one
or more of the Judges of the Court of Common
Pleas.   The powers and management of these courts
remained much the same until the beginning of the
present century.

The County of Worcester was incorporated by an
act passed on the 2nd of April, 1731, to take effect
the 10th of the following July.   The first session of
the inferior courts was held on the 10th of August,
on which occasion the Rev. John Prentice of Lancaster preached a sermon from the appropriate text,
2nd Chronicles, xix., 6 and 7.

The Act of Incorporation of the County is here
printed:

[1] Washburn's Judicial History of Massachusetts.

An Act

for erecting, granting and making a County in the Inland Parts of this Province, to be called the County of *Worcester*, and for establishing Courts of Justice within the same.

BE it enacted by his Excellency the Governour, Council and Representatives in General Court assembled, and by the Authority of the same, That the Towns and Places hereafter named and expressed, *That is to say, Worcester, Lancaster, Westborough, Shrewsbury, Southborough, Leicester, Rutland,* and *Lunenburg,* all in the County of *Middlesex; Mendon, Woodstock, Oxford, Sutton,* (including *Hassanamisco) Uxbridge,* and the Land lately granted to several Petitioners of *Medfield,* all in the County of *Suffolk; Brookfield* in the County of *Hampshire,* and the South Town laid out to the *Narragansett* Soldiers ; and all other Lands lying within the said Townships, with the Inhabitants thereon, shall from and after the tenth Day of *July,* which will be in the Year of our Lord One Thousand seven Hundred and thirty one, be and remain one intire and distinct County, by the Name of *Worcester,* of which *Worcester* to be the County or Shire Town : And the Said County to have, use and enjoy all such Powers, Priviledges and Immunities, as by Law other Counties within this Province have and do enjoy.

And be it further enacted by the Authority aforesaid, That there shall be held and kept within the said County of Worcester yearly and in every Year, at the Times and Place in this Act hereafter expressed, a Court of General Sessions of the Peace, and an Inferiour Court of Common Pleas, to sit at Worcester on the second Tuesdays of *May* and *August,* and the first Tuesdays of *November* and *February* yearly and in every Year, until this Court shall otherwise order : *Also,* That there shall be held and kept at Worcester within the said County of Worcester yearly and in every Year until this Court shall otherwise order, a Superiour Court of Judicature Court of Assize and General Goal

Delivery, to sit on the Wednesday immediately preceeding the Time by Law appointed for the holding of the said Superior Court of Judicature Court of Assize and General Goal Delivery at *Springfield*, within and for the County of *Hampshire:* And the Justices of the said Court of General Sessions of the Peace, Inferiour Court of Common Pleas, Superiour Court of Judicature, Court of Assize and General Goal Delivery respectively, who are or shall be thereunto lawfully commissioned and appointed, shall have, hold, use, exercise and enjoy all and singular the Powers which are by Law already given and granted unto them, within any other Counties of the Province, where a Court of General Sessions of the Peace, Inferiour Court of Common Pleas, Superiour Court of Judicature, Court of Assize and General Goal Delivery, are already established.

Provided, That all Writs, Suits, Plaints, Process, Appeals, Reviews, Recognizances, or any other Matters or Things which now are, or at any Time before the said tenth Day of *July*, shall be depending in the Law within any Part of the said County of Worcester; and also all Matters and Things which now are, or at any Time before the said tenth of *July*, shall be depending before the Judges of Probate within any Part of the said County of Worcester, shall be heard, tried, proceeded upon and determined in the Counties of *Suffolk*, *Middlesex* and *Hampshire* respectively, where the same are or shall be returnable or depending, and have or shall have Day or Days.

Provided also, That nothing in this Act contained, shall be construed to disannul, defeat, or make void any Deeds or Conveyances of Lands, lying in the said County of Worcester, where the same are, or shall be before the said tenth of *July*, recorded in the Register's office of the respective Counties where such Lands do now lie; but that all such Deeds or Conveyances so recorded, shall be held good and valid as they would have been had not this Act been made.

And be it further enacted by the Authority aforesaid, That the Justices of the Court of General Sessions of the Peace at their first Meeting in the said County of Worcester, shall have full Power and Authority to appoint some meet Person within the said County of Worcester to be Register of Deeds and Conveyances within the same, who shall be sworn to the faithful Discharge of his Trust in the said Office, and shall continue to hold and exercise the same according to the Directions of the Law, until some Person be elected by the Freeholders of the said County of Worcester, who are hereby impowered to choose such Person on the first Thursday of *September* next ensuing, by the Methods in the Law already prescribed, to take upon him that Trust : And until such Register shall be so appointed by the said Justices and sworn, all Deeds and Conveyances of Lands lying within any Part of the County of Worcester, which shall be recorded in the Register's Office of the respective Counties where such Lands do now lie, shall be held and deemed good and valid to all Intents and Purposes as to the recording thereof.

And be it further enacted by the Authority aforesaid, That the Methods, Directions and Proceedings by Law provided as well for the electing and choosing a Register of Deeds and Conveyances as a County Treasurer, which Officers shall be appointed in the same Manner as is by Law already provided, on the first Thursday of *September* next, and also for the bringing forward and trying any Actions, Causes, Pleas or Suits both Civil and Criminal in the several Counties of this Province and Courts of Judicature within the same, and choosing of Jurors to serve at the Courts of Justice, shall extend and be attended, observed and put in Practice within the said County of Worcester, and by the Courts of Justice within the same : Any Law, Usage or Custom to the contrary notwithstanding.

Provided always, That the Inhabitants of the several Towns and Places herein before enumerated and set off a distinct County, shall pay their Proportion to any County Rates or Taxes already made and granted, in the same Manner as they would have done, had not this Act been made.

RECORDS

Court of General Sessions

OF THE PEACE.

A Copy of the

General Commission for the Peace

for the County of Worcester

1731

(Seal) George the Second by the Grace of God of Great Brittain France and Ireland King Defender of the Faith &c.ᵗ

To our Trusty and well beloved John Chandler Joseph Wilder William Ward William Jennison Daniel Taft John Chandler Junʳ Benjamin Willard Samuel Wright Josiah Willard Joseph Dwight Samuel Dudley Henry Lee and Nahum Ward Esqʳˢ Greeting——

Know ye that we have assigned you and every of you our Justices to Keep our Peace in our County of Worcester within our Province of the Massachusetts Bay in New England, and to Keep and Cause to be Kept the laws and Ordinances made for the good of the Peace and for the Conservation of the Same and for the Quiet Rule and Government of our People in our Said County in all and every the articles thereof according to the force fform and effect of the Same and to Chastise and Punish all Persons offending against the form of those laws & ordinances or any of them in the County aforesaid or according to the form of those laws and ordinances Shall be fitt to be done, and to Cause to Come before you or any of you, all those thatt Shall breake the peace or attempt anything against the Same, or that Shall threaten any our

3

People in their person or in burning their houses to find Sufficient Security for the peace or for the good behaviour towards us and our people and if they shall refuse to find such security then to cause them to be Kept Safe in Prison untill they shall find the same and to do and perform in the County aforesaid all and whatsoever according to the laws and Ordinances of our Province aforesaid or any of them, Justices of the Peace may or ought to do & perform and we Command you and every of you that you Deligently intend the Keeping of the Peace and of the laws and Ordinances aforesaid ; and that at such certain days and places as are or shall be by law Stated and appointed (whereof any of you The said John Chandler Joseph Wilder William Ward & William Jennison always to be one) enquire by the Oaths of good and Carefull men of our Said County by whom the Truth may be the better Known of all and all manner of Thefts, Trespases, Riots, Routs, and unlawfull assemblys whatsoever, and all and singular other misdeeds and offences of which by law Justices of the peace in their Generall Sessions may or ought to Inquire, by whomsoever or howsoever done and Perpetrated, or which shall hereafter happen howsoever to be done or attempted in the County aforesaid, Contrary to the form of the laws and Ordinances aforesaid, made for the Common good of our province aforesaid and the People thereof, and to Inspect all Indictments So before you taken or to be Taken, and to make and Continue the Process thereupon against all and every person or persons so Indicted before Shall hereafter happen to be Indicted before you untill they be apprehended render themselves or be outlawed, and to hear and Determine all & Singular the said Thefts, Trespasses, Riots, Routs, unlawfull assemblys, and all and Singular Other the premises, and to do therein as to Justice appertaineth according to the laws Statutes and Ordinances aforesaid ; Saving to us the amerciaments and Other things thereof to us belonging ; and we likewise Command that at such days and places as are or shall be by law appointed for holding a Court of General Sessions of the peace as aforesaid and Such and So many good and lawfull men of the County aforesaid you cause to come before you or any Three or more of you as aforesaid, by whom the Truth in the premises may be Known and Inquired of; In testimony whereof we have Caused the Publicke Seal of our Province aforesaid to be hereunto affixed

Witness Jonathan Belcher Esqʳ our Capᵗ Generall and Governour in Chief in and over our Said Province at Boston the thirtyth day of June 1731 in the fifth year of our reigne

J Belcher

By order of the Govʳ with the advice and Consent of the Councill   J. Willard *Secry.*

John Chandler John Chandler Junʳ Joseph Dwight and Samuel Dudley Esqrs

Sworn in Councill July 1ˢᵗ 1731   J Willard *Secy*

Joseph Wilder William Ward William Jennison Daniell Taft Samuel Wright Josiah Willard Henry Lee & Nahum Ward Esq's Sworn by Dedimus from his Exce'y the Govʳ before us

John Chandler   John Chandler Jr   Joseph Dwight

A true Copy from the Originall Commission

attesᵗ John Chandler Jr Cler Pac.

NOTES.

Of the persons named in the foregoing Commission, John Chandler, Joseph Wilder, William Ward and William Jennison were the Justices of the Court of Common Pleas for the County. JOHN CHANDLER of Woodstock, (now in Connecticut but formerly included in Worcester County) was a man of considerable prominence. He was the first Judge of Probate for the County; Chief Justice of the Court of Common Pleas, and of the Court of General Sessions; Colonel of the regiment of militia; Representative, and a member of his Majesty's Council. He died in 1743.

JOSEPH WILDER was a prominent citizen of Lancaster, and a man of influence in the County. He became Chief Justice on the death of John Chandler in 1743.

WILLIAM WARD of Southborough was born in 1680 and died (probably) in 1745. He was a Colonel of the militia.

WILLIAM JENNISON lived in Worcester, where he held various offices of trust. He died in 1741.

Of the Justices of the Peace, Daniel Taft resided in Mendon ; Benjamin Willard in Hassanamisco, now Grafton; Samuel Wright in Rutland; Josiah Willard in Lunenburg; and Henry Lee in Worcester.

Nahum Ward of Shrewsbury was a lawyer of some note, and subsequently became one of the Judges of the Court of Common Pleas. He was father of Major General Artemas Ward of revolutionary fame.

John Chandler Junior was born in Woodstock in 1693, and removed to Worcester in 1731. He was Clerk of the Courts, Register of Deeds, etc.; and succeeded to most of the offices held by his father. He died in 1763.

Joseph Dwight was born in Hatfield in 1703, and graduated at Harvard College in 1722. He lived for some years in Brookfield, and represented that town in the Provincial Legislature. He was Speaker of the House of Representatives in 1749, and at one time a member of the Council. Distinguished for his military talents he attained the rank of Brigadier General, and for his bravery at the siege of Louisburg, where he commanded a regiment, was publicly commended by Sir William Pepperell. Dwight was Judge of the Court of Common Pleas for the County of Worcester from 1743 to 1750, and afterwards held the same office in Berkshire County. He died at Great Barrington in 1765.

Samuel Dudley was one of the largest land owners of Sutton, and a man of influence and prominence. He was born in Concord in 1666, and died in 1775 at the great age of 109 years.

WORCESTER ss

Memorandum Worcester Aug^st 12th 1731

Att ye first meeting of the Justices of the County aforesaid, John Chandler Junr Esq was appointed Register of Deeds for Said County and Sworn to the faithfull Discharge of the Said Trust before all the Justices by the Honble John Chandler Esqr The first Justice

Attestator   John Chandler J^r Cle Pac :

August 13th Mr Jonathan Houghton of Lancaster was appointed & Sworn County Treasurer

Attest   John Chandler J^r Clck

Same day John Chandler Junr Esqr Register of Deeds gave bond to the County Treas^r with two Suretys in five hundred, for his acting faithfully as Register of Deeds This was done by order of the Justices   Attes^t John Chandler J^r Cler Pac

WORCESTER ss *Anno Regni Regis Georgij Secundi nunc Magniæ Brittaniæ Franciæ et Hiberniæ Quinto*

Att a Court of Generall Sessions of the Peace held at Worcester for and within the County of Worcester The Second Tuesday of Augst being the Tenth day of Said Month Annoq Dom 1731

JUSTICES PRESENT

JOHN CHANDLER		SAMUELL WRIGHT	
JOSEPH WILDER		JOSIAH WILLARD	
WILLIAM WARD	Quo :	JOSEPH DWIGHT	
WILLIAM JENNISON	Esq^{rs}	SAMUEL DUDLEY	Esq^{rs}
DANIEL TAFT		HENRY LEE	
JOHN CHANDLER JUN^r		NAHUM WARD	

CORONERS, Mr Joseph Wilder Mr Seth Chapin Junr Mr Joseph Wright

Grand Jurors that were Returned & Served are as follows vizt

Worcester	Mr Gershom Rice	Lancaster	Mr Ebenezer Wilder
Mendon	Mr James Keith	Woodstock	Mr Joseph Baron
Brookfield	Mr Joseph Banister	Westboro'	Mr Thomas Rice foreman
Oxford	Mr Isaac Lernard	Sutton	Parcivall Hall
Leicester	Mr Daniell Denney	Southboro'	Mr John Woods
Shrewsbury	Mr David How	Ruttland	Mr Joseph Stevens
Uxbridge	Mr Robert Taft	Lunenburg	Mr Edward Hartwell

Each Served Two Days

Phillip Chase of Sutton in ye County of Worcester Husbandman
and Others Came into Court and Complained that Solomon Johnson Resident in Said Shrewsbury Gent in the Night following the
11th Instant was Guilty of ye Breach of ye peace by Stricking him
the Said Chase on the face with his hand and of Speaking Insult-
ing and threating words, The Said Solomon Johnson appeared
before ye Court and pleaded not Guilty and in the Court behaved
himself in a very Insolent Rude and unbecoming manner both to
the Court & Officers thereof Capt Thomas Baker and Said Chase
were Sworn as Evidences in the Case and after due Examination
the Case being fully heard the Said Solomon Johnson is Judged to
be Guilty of the Breach of ye peace in Striking Said Chase and
useing threatning words and thereupon order that for Said offence
he pay as a fine to our Sovereign Lord the King &c Twenty Shillings and for his Said Rude and Insulting Behaviour he also pay as
a fine to our said Lord the King the Sum of fourty Shillings that
he give bond with Two Suretys for his peacable and good behaviour till the next Court of General Sessions of
the peace to be holden at Worcester &c the first
Tuesday of November next vizt The Said Solomon
Johnson as principall In ye Sum of fifty pounds &
the Suretys in Twenty five pound Each and Pay Costs & Stand
Committed till Sentance be Performed Costs Taxed at one pounds
nine Shillings The Said Solomon Johnson appealed from this
Sentance unto the Court of assize and Generall Goal Delivery to
be holden at Worcester the 4th Wednesday of September next and
Entered into Recognizance with Two Suretys to
prossecute his appeal to Effect and to abide and
perform ye order or Sentance of Said Court thereon
and to be of ye Good behaviour in the meantime

Solomon Johnson principal 50 l / Benjn Townsend & Joseph Crosby Surety 25 l Each

Chase & Baker Recognized in 5 l Each to appear as witnesses

Joseph Crosby of Worcester in the County of Worcester Sadler,
was bound over to this Court by Mr Justice Jenison on the Complaint of Isaac Miller of Shrewsbury In Said County Husbandman
for abusing & Striking him &c : as by the Complaint & writt will

appear said Miller being bound by Recognizance to prosecute his Complaint the Case was delivered to the Grand Jury who Did upon their Oaths Return Ignoramus, whereupon Said Crosby was Delivered from his Recognizance, and the Court adjudged Said Miller to pay Cost of Court Taxed at four pounds nineteen Shillings & Tenpence

John Hazeltine of Sutton in the County of Worcester Husbandman upon ye Complaint of Christian Indian Woman Widdow of George Misco late of Hassanamisco, for his Said Hazeltines Selling Strong Drink to ye Indians Contrary To law[1] &c‘ was bound over to this Court by Mr Justice Jenison to answer to Said Complaint   The Court having Considered the Case order that his Recognizance be Continued to the next Court of Generall Sessions of ye peace to be holden at Worcester for ye Said County of Worcester ye fs‘ Tuesday in Novembr next

And then ye Court was adjourned to ye 4th Wednesday in Sepr Next att Ten oClock in ye forenoon, To ye House of William Jenison Esq in Worcester

                              attestr   John Chandler Jr Cler pac

---

[1] See Note on page 28.

4

Att a Court of Generall Sessions of ye Peace held at Worcester for and within the County of Worcester by adjournment on Wednesday the 22^d day of September 1731

PRESENT

John Chandler Joseph Wilder William Ward & Wm Jenison Esq^{rs} Jus^t of ye pea^s & Quo :

John Chandler Junr Samuell Wright Joseph Dwight Samuel Dudley & Henry Lee Esqs J p

———

The Several Towns having made Return of their Several Choices for a Register of Deeds and a County Treasurer according to law, William Ward John Chandler Junr & Joseph Dwight Esqrs were appointed a Committee to view & Sort the Same and Report To ye Court who were Chosen, The Said Committee Having Sorted the votes of the freeholders for a Register of Deeds made Report that John Chandler Junr Esq was Chosen by a very great majority of Votes The Said Committee having Sorted the Votes Returned for a County Treas^r made Return that Mr Jonathan Houghton was Chosen by a great majority of votes The Said persons were Respectively Sworn to the faithfull Discharge of their Respective offices in Court and the Register of Deeds gave Bond with Suretys according to Law

Attes^t John Chandler Jun Cler pac

———

The Court order that a House of the following Dimensions be built at the Charge of the County for a Prison House and Prison namely Thirty six feet Long Seventeen feet wide fourteen feet post,

The Prison End to be Studed with Timber of Five Inch & four Inch and placed within five inches of one another and that the Joyce be of the same bigness and placed at the Same Distance and that it be planked within and without with good plank Spiked on, and that there be a Dungeon under the same and that the Other End of the House be finished after the usuall manner of Dwelling Houses and that there be a Sutable Prison Yard of Twenty feet Deep & thirty feet Long against the House made with boards nailed To Sutable posts about Eight or Ten feet high that there be a Chimney built in ye Dwelling part with a fire Room below and one in the Chamber—and William Jenison Henry Lee and Nahum Ward Esqrs are appointed a Committee to See the work be done and at as Cheap a lay as may be and it is further ordered that the Said Prison House &c̃t be Sett not Southward of the land given by William Jenison Esq to the County nor Northward of the Reverend m^r Burrs Barn and on the Westerly Side ye Highway in the most Convenient place

The Court order that untill the prison be built That the House of William Jenison Esq by his consent be the Prison and that a Sutable Cage be built in y^e Back part thereof and that the prison yard Shall Extend Twenty feet on the South Side and East End thereof and so far on the North Side and West end thereof as shall Include y^e House & Office. The Court also order a County Tax or assesment on y^e Several Towns amounting to 303$^£$: 5„ 4^d being a Tax eaquall with the previous Tax and That the Clerk send out warrants accordingly Requiring the Selectmen or assessors of each Town to assess the Same and that it be Collected and paid into the County Treasury at or before the last day of march next for defraying the Charges of the County

NOTE.

PENALTY FOR SELLING STRONG DRINK TO THE INDIANS.—(See page 25.) In 1693 the General Court passed "An Act for the better Rule and Government of the Indians in their Several Places and Plantations, *To the Intent that the* Indians *may be forwarded in Civility and Christianity; and other Vices the more effectually Suppressed amongst them:*"

One clause of this act was:

"——That no Person or Persons whosoever, shall directly or indirectly, sell, truck, barter or give to any Indian, any strong Beer, Ale, Cyder, Perry, Rum, Brandy, or other strong Liquors, by what Name or Names soever called or known; on Pain of forfeiting the sum of *forty Shillings* for every Pint; and proportionably for any greater or lesser Quantity so sold, truck'd bartered, given or delivered to any Indian directly or indirectly as aforesaid; upon Conviction thereof before a Justice of the Peace where the Penalty does not exceed *forty Shillings*; and if it exceed that Sum, at the Sessions of the Peace to be holden for the same County where the Offence is committed: one Moiety of all such Forfeitures to be unto their Majesties, for and towards the Support of the Government; and the other Moiety to him or them that shall inform and prosecute the same by Bill, Plaint, or Information. And if the Offender be unable, or shall not forthwith pay and satisfy the said Penalty or Forfeiture, then to be committed to the Goal of the County; there to remain until he pay and satisfy the same, or suffer two months Imprisonment.

"*Provided,* This Act shall not be intended or extend to restrain any Act of Charity for relieving any Indian (*bona fide*) in any sudden Exigent or Faintness or Sickness, not to exceed one or two Drams; or by Prescription of some Physician in writing, or by allowance of a Justice of Peace."

The accusation and affirmation of an Indian were received as evidence.

Intoxication in Indians was punished by fine or whipping; and liquor found in their possession was seized.

WORCESTER ss *Anno Regni Regis Georgij Secundi nunc Magniæ Brittaniæ Franciæ et Hiberniæ Quinto*⟳

A tt a Court of General Sessions of yᵉ peace held at Worcester for & within yᵉ County of Worcester yᵉ 1ˢᵗ Tuesday of Novʳ being yᵉ 2ᵈ day of Said Month Annoq Dom 1731

John Chandler Esq Joseph Wilder Esq Wᵐ Ward Esq Wᵐ Jenison Esq of yᵉ Quoᵐ

Jno Chandler Jʳ Samˡ Wright Joseph Dwight Samuel Dudley Henry Lee & Nahum Ward Esq J p :

The Same Grand Jury attended as did yᵉ first Court, and Attended one day

————

The Court order That the floors in yᵉ Prison End of yᵉ House ordered to be built at the last Court be laid with plank and that there be a Cellar under yᵉ Same and an oven in the Chimney and it is left to the Committee to plank or board yᵉ Outsides as they think proper

———.

The Reverend Mʳ David Parsons of Leicester Preferred a Petition or Complaint to this Court Shewing that in yᵉ year 1721 he accepted the Call of the Church and Town of Leicester to yᵉ Gospell ministry among them with an Incouragement of an Honˡ

Support of Seventy five pounds &ct—from year to year In which
Service yᵉ Said Petitioner has Continued Ever Since according to
his poor Capacity Heartyly endeavoured to be faithfull, butt that
through the negligence of the Town he has not Recᵈ any part of
his dues from them since march : 1730 butt that they have been
wholly Deficient Since that time praying for Reliefe according to
the Directions of yᵉ good and wholesome laws of this province,
which petition being duly Considered The Court order and Direct
the Selectmen of yᵉ Town of Leicester be by warrant under the
Clerks hand Convented before yᵉ Court of General Sessions of yᵉ
peace to be holden at Worcester for and within the County of
Worcester on the first Tuesday of February next To answer To
Said Petition [1]

JURY

Capt Jonas Rice

Capt Richard Moore

Mr Epm Child

Mr Bezalcel Sawyer

Mr Richard Ward

Mr Comfort Barns

Mr Perez Rice

Mr Peter Smith

Mr Wm Brown

Mr Isaac Amsden

Mr Eli Ball

Mr Nathan Dyke

John Hazeltines Recognizance being Continued
to this Court by which he was bound To answer
to the Complaint of Christian Indian Widdow
of George Misco &ct for His said Hazeltines
Selling Strong Drink to yᵉ Indians Contrary to
law &ct The Said John Hazeltine appeared in
Court and to yᵉ Complaint Pleaded not Guilty
and put himself on his Country for Tryall   The
Complainant also appearing in Court affirming
That the said John Hazeltine was Guilty of Selling Great Quantitys of Strong [drink] to Indians
and the Case after a full hearing was Committed
to yᵉ Jury who were Sworn to Try yᵉ Same according to law who Returned yᵉ following Ver-
dict vizᵗ We find the Defendant Guilty of giving order for one
Jill of Rum to be delivered to an Indian   Its therefore considered
by the Court that the said John Hazeltine pay a fine of Ten Shillings one half to his majesty the other half to the Informer and pay
Costs Taxed at Seven pound nine Shillings & Two pence, which

---

[1] See Note, next page.

fine and Costs he paid down in Court and the Same was Delivered
to the Respective persons to whom ye Same is Due : Excepting y^e
Kings part which is in ye hands of ye Clerk.

and then the Court was adjourned without day

Attes^t John Chandler J^r Cler p^c :

memorandum   a By law of the Town of Woodstock was first
approved of ye Court [   ]

att   Jno Chandler Jr Cle pac

NOTE.

CASE OF THE REVEREND DAVID PARSONS.—(See page 29.) The Rev.
David Parsons, whose troubles frequently claimed the attention of this Court,
was a brother of the Rev. Joseph Parsons, a large land holder (but not a
resident) of Leicester. They were grandsons of Joseph Parsons, the emi-
grant, who was in Springfield in 1636. David was born at Northampton,
February 1, 1680; and graduated at Harvard College in 1705. He became
the minister of Malden in 1708; and in 1721, in consequence, it is said, of
some difficulty with his people, he accepted the call of the Church of Leicester and removed to that town. The connection then formed proved unfortu-
nate in the extreme : a serious quarrel began and kept the town in tumult
for twelve or more years. Blame probably rests with both parties. The
principal ground of the minister's complaint was the nonpayment of his sal-
ary. The town in extenuation declared that they were unable through poverty to meet his requirements; and offered other excuses to put off his de-
mands. The fact seems to have been that Mr. Parsons was not agreeable
to a large portion of his parishioners, and they probably did not exert themselves with proper zeal to secure his support, hoping that their neglect would
drive him to resign his charge. He, with the common understanding of the
time that a settlement was for life, resisted these attempts and slights to the
utmost.

Mr. Parsons petitioned the General Court for relief, and entered com-
plaints from time to time in the Courts. Counter petitions were presented,
and at one time the General Court passed an act relieving the town from
his support, which Governor Belcher vetoed. A dangerous schism in the
church and town followed. Finally the quarrel became so scandalous that
in the interest of good order, other towns interfered; and in 1735, a Council

was called by mutual agreement, and the result was the dismission of Mr.
Parsons. He left the place, but returned after a year or two, and resided
there until his death which occurred in 1743. He brought suits against the
town after his return.

He carried his resentment against his former parishioners to the grave;
and according to his request was buried in the center of an open field owned
by him, at a distance from the general burial ground. In the course of time
his grave was plowed over. The stone was used in building a chimney for a
house in Leicester; and a few years since the inscription was seen on the
inside wall of an ash hole. It was as follows:

In memory of

Rev. Mr. DAVID PARSONS

who after many years of

Hard Labour and Suffering

was laid here

Oct. 12, 1743

aged sixty-three

An account of the Parsons controversy will be found in Washburn's History of Leicester.

WORCESTER ss *Anno Regni Regis Georgij Secundi nunc Magniæ Brittaniæ Franciæ et Hiberniæ Quinto*

Att a Court of General Sessions of the peace held at Worcester for & within the County of Worcester the first Tuesday of February being the first day of Said Month Annoq Dom 1731

JUSTICES PRESENT

John Chandler	⎫ Esqrs Jus	Josiah Willard	⎫
Joseph Wilder	⎬ of Peace	Joseph Dwight	⎪
William Ward	⎪ &	Samuel Dudley	⎬ Esqrs Justices
William Jenison	⎭ Quorum	Henry Lee	⎪
		Nahum Ward	⎭
Daniel Taft	⎱ Esqrs		
John Chandler Junr	⎰ Justices		

Names of the Grand Jurors who served this Court

viz:

Mr Thomas Rice foreman	Mr Isaac Learned	Mr Daniel How
Mr Gershom Rice	Mr Parcivall Hall	Mr Joseph Stevens
Mr Ephraim Wilder	Mr Daniel Denny	Mr Robert Taft
Mr James Keith	Mr John Woods	Mr Edward Hart-
Mr Joseph Banister		[well

Each attended Two days

5

Whereas at a Court of Generall Sessions of the Peace Held at
Worcester for the County of Worcester by adjournment on Wednesday the 22ᵈ day of September last past The Justices Then ordered a Prison or Goal to be built, and appointed a Committee to
See the Same Effected and Nothing as yett being done in the af-
faire This Court now order that John Chandler Junʳ be added to
said Committee and that they do with all Convenient Speed at the
Charge of the County Build & Erect a good Sufficient and Substantiall Prison or Goal with a house to the Same att the place
where it was formerly Stated in Worcester, of the following Dimensions In Lieu of that formerly ordered to be built namely
fourty one feet Long Eighteen feet wide and Eight feet Studd that
that part which is for a Goal or Prison be Eighteen feett Square
and made of good Substantiall White Oak Timber That the Studs
be four Inches thick five Inches broad and placed within five
Inches one of another all round the Said Goal that there be a
lower Summer[1] & floor of Joyce and a Chamber Summer & floor
of Joyce The Joyce of the Same bigness with the Studds and placed
the Same Distance asunder, That it [be] planked within Side with
full Inch & half Plank and with out Side with full Two Inch Plank
and to be spiked on so as to every plank of Twelve Inches wide
against Every Studd there be Two Spikes at least that the floor be
of Two Inch Plank Spiked on and the lower floor lined with boards
That there be Sutable Grates Doors and bolts & Locks to it & Di-
visions so as to make three Rooms in all and a Sufficient Dungeon
under the Same built as yᵉ Committee may think proper That
the other Part of the House be finished in all Regards after the
manner of a Dwelling house Compleat with a Chimney Cellar and
oven The Ruff of the whole house to be of the fashion Called
Gamber Ruff   the out Sides & Ruff to be boarded Claboarded
& Shingled as usuall and the Prison or Goal also to be Claboarded
save that Round the bottom of the whole yᵗ may be boarded about
Two feet high as yᵉ Committee may order and that there be made
adjoining to the Goal or Prison a Yard of Eight feet high with
boards to be Thirty feet Long and Twenty feet Wide, and the

---

[1] A central floor timber, also called a summer-tree.

Committee or major part of them are hereby Impowered to lett the Same out To Such person or persons as may appear to perform the Service or to have it Done in Such other manner as they may think proper, and in the mean time and in lieu of the prison already appointed this Court order and appoint that the Cage (as so Called) already built be Removed to the Chamber of the house of Daniel Haywood in Worcester and be the Goal till Said Chamber be Sutably finished for a Goal and that then Said Chamber be ye Goal for Said County and Said Cage remain as one of the appartments thereof, untill the Prison &c^t now agreed upon be built and that Twenty feet on Ends & back side the House and four perch on the South Side the House be accounted the Prison Yard.

and it is Further ordered by this Court that the Clerk doe and he is hereby ordered to Issue out a Warrant Directed To the Sheriff[1] Requiring him to Remove all Such Prisoners as may be in the Goal heretofore appointed to the Goal now appointed,[2]

Which was done the 3^d Day of Feby Instant

———

A List of the Presentments made by ye Grand Jurers to this Court vizt The Grand Jury for the body of the S^d County do present [   ] The Towns of Worcester Brookfield Uxbridge Southborough & Lunenburg Each and Every of them for their not being provided with Stocks as the Law Requires[3]

2^ndly The Towns of Brookfield Leicester Southborough and Lunenburg Each and Every of them for their not being provided with weights & measures as the law Requires.

3^ly The Town of Rutland for not being provided with weights as the law Requires.

4^thly The Towns of Uxbridge and Southborough and Each of them for not being provided with a writing and Reading School master as the law Requires.[4]

5^thly John Jordan of Brookfield Husbandman and Submitt Jordan of Brookfield ye wife of the said John Jordan Housewife and

---

[1] The first Sheriff of the County was Daniel Gookin, son of the Maj. Gen.
[2] [3] [4] See Notes at the end of the Record of this term of the Court.

William Cratten of Uxbridge Husbandman and Easter Cratten of Uxbridge aforesaid wife of yᵉ Said William Cratten Housewife Each and every of them for the Sin of Fornication[1]

6ᵗʰˡʸ   John Hastings of Lunenburg Husbandman Jonathan Wheeler and Jonathan Moore Junr Husbandmen and both of Lancaster and all in the Said County Each and all of them for their absenting themselves from yᵉ Publick worship of God for more than one month[2] last past, all which things are against the peace of our Sovereign Lord the King his Crown and Dignity

Joseph Dwight att pro Reg"

Billa Vera   Thomas Rice foreman   ·

Jonathan Wheler of Lancaster in yᵉ County of Worcester Husbandman being presented by the Grand Jurors of our Sovereign Lord the King for that he the said Jonathan has absented himself from the Publick worship of God for more than one month last past against the peace of our Sovereign Lord the King his Crown and Dignity, the said Jonathan Wheler Came into Court and Pleaded not Guilty putt himself upon Tryall by the Court the matter being duly considered it is the opinion of the Court that the said Jonathan Wheler is not Guilty of absenting himself from the Publick worship of God for more than one month last past & therefore order that the said Jonathan Wheler be Dismissed paying the Cost of his prosecution Taxed at Twelve Shillings & Sixpence from which Judgment the Said Jonathan Wheler appealed to the next Court of assize and General Goal Delivery to be holden for this County at Worcester within and for said County on the Wednesday Immediately preceeding the time by law appointed for the holding yᵉ said Court of assize and Generall Goal Delivery at Springfield within and for the County of Hampshire In September next and entered into Recognizance with Two Suretys as the law Directs for prosecuting his appeal with Effect and to abide and perform the order or Sentence of Court thereon.

Cost pᵈ & appeal withdrawn

---

[1] [2] See Notes at the end of the Record of this term of the Court.

Jonathan Moore of Lancaster in the County of Worcester Husbandman being presented by the Grandjurors for the body of said County For that he the Said Jonathan Moore has absented himself from the Publick worship of God for more than one month last past, against the peace of our Sovereign Lord the King his Crown and Dignity. The said Jonathan Moore came into Court & Pleaded not Guilty & putt himself upon Tryall by the Court and the Court Taking the Case into their Consideration & having maturely Considered thereof are of opinion that the Said Jonathan Moore is not Guilty of absenting himself from the Publick Worship of God for more than one month last past and therefore order that the said Jonathan Moore pay the Cost of his prosecution Taxed at Twelve Shillings and Six pence ; from which Judgment the said Jonathan Moore appealed to the next Court of assize and Generall Goal Delivery to be holden at Worcester within and for the County of Worcester on the Wednesday Imediately preceeding the time by law appointed for the holding the said Court of assize & Generall Goal Delivery at Springfield within and for the County of Hampshire In September next and Entered into Recognizance with Two Suretys as the law Directs for prosecuting his appeal with Effeçt and to abide & perform yᵉ order or Sentance of Court thereon

Cost paid & appeal withdrawn

Benjamin Whitney of Lancaster, In the County of Worcester Husbandman being bound over by way of Recognizance to this Court by mʳ Justice Wilder to answer for his being Guilty of the Sin of fornication, appeared in Court & Pleaded Guilty whereupon the Court ordered that he pay as a fine The Sum of Twenty Shillings & Cost 2/6 which he paid Down in Court and his Recognizance Cancelled

---

A Petition of William King and Others Inhabitants of the Town of Sutton Shewing that they are of the perswasion of those Called

annabaptists praying they may obtain the favour granted them by
the laws of the province made in ye first & Second years and in
the third year of his present majestys Reigne.[1]   and that the Court
would appoint Some meet persons to bring into this Court a list of
all such persons within Said Town of Sutton that profess themselves to be of the Said Denomination and usually attend Such
meetings according to ye law.   Read & being Duly Considered
Ordered that Cap^tt William King & m^r Benjamin marsh be Impowered to take and bring into this Court at the Sessions In august
next a list of all Persons within the Town of Sutton that are of the
Denomination Called annabaptists and usually attend Such meeting That the Court may advise and act thereupon agreeable to law.

————

A Petition of Thomas Green and Others Inhabitants of the Town
of Leicester Shewing that they are of the perswasion or Denomination of those Commonly Called annabaptists praying that they may
obtain the favour and Priviledge Granted to them by the laws of
the province made in the first & Second years and in the third year
of the Reign of his present majestys &ct and that the Court would
appoint Some meet persons to bring into this Court a list of all
such persons within the Town of Leicester that profess themselves
to be of Said Denomination and usually attend such meetings according to the law

Read and the same being Duly Considered Ordered that m^r
Thomas Green & m^r Daniell Denney be Impowered to take and
bring Into this Court at the Session in august next a list of all per-
sons within the Town of Leicester that are of the Denomination
Called annabaptists and usually attend Such meetings that the
Court may advise and act thereupon agreeable to law

————

Benjamin Wheler of Lancaster in the County of Worcester Husbandman being bound over to this Court by m^r Justice Wilder to
answer to his presentment by the Grandjurors of our Sovereign

————

[1] See Notes at the end of the Record of this term of the Court.

Lord the King for his neglecting to attend the Publick worship of God for more than one month last past which is against ye good and wholesome laws of this province and against the peace of our Sovereign the King his Crown & Dignity Came into Court & to his presentment Pleaded not Guilty & put himself upon Tryall by the Court The Case being fully Considered The Court are of opinion that the Said Benjamin Wheler is not Guilty of neglecting to attend the Publick Worship of God for more than one month last past as Sett forth in the Said presentment and therefore order that the Said Benjamin Wheeler be Dismisst from his bonds & pay the Cost of his prosecution Taxed at one pound Six Shillings & Sixpence from which Judgment the Said Benjamin Wheler appealed to the next Court of assize and Generall Goal Delivery to be holden at Worcester within and for the County of Worcester on the Wednesday Imediately preceding the time by law appointed for the holding the said Court of Assize and Generall Goal Delivery at Springfield within and for the County of Hampshire In September next and entered into Recognizance with two Suretys as the law directs for his prosecuting his appeal with Effect and to abide & perform the order or Sentance of Court thereon

Cost paid appeal withdrawn

Mary Moore Housewife of lancaster in the County of Worcester wife of Jonathan Moore Junr of Said Lancaster being bound over to this Court by m^r Justice Wilder to answer to her presentment by the Grandjurors of our Sovereign Lord the King for Said County for her neglecting to attend the Publick worship of God for more than one month last past, which is against the good and wholesome laws of this province and against the Peace of our Sovereign lord the King his Crown and Dignity, Came into Court & to her presentment pleaded not Guilty and put herself upon Tryall by the Court, The Case being fully heard & Duly Considered the Court are of opinion that the said Mary Moore is not Guilty of neglecting to attend the Publick worship of God for more than one month last past as sett forth in the presentment and therefore order that

the Said Moore be Dismisst from her bonds and pay the Cost of
her prosecution Taxed at one pound Eleven Shillings & Three
pence from which Judgment the Said Mary Moore appealed to the
next Court of assize and Generall Goal Delivery to be holden at
Worcester within and for the County of Worcester on the Wednesday Imediately preceeding the time by law appointed for the holding the said Court of assize and Generall Goal Delivery at Springfield within and for the County of Hampshire In September next
and entered into Recognizance with two Suretys as the law directs
for her prosecuteing her appeal with Effect and to abide & perform ye order or Sentance of Court thereupon

Cost paid appeal withdrawn

David Parsons of Leicester in ye County of Worcester Clerk [1]
Complainant versus the Selectmen of Leicester aforesaid Defend^{ts}.
&c^t as pr the writt & Petition on file may appear. The Selectmen
desiring the Case may be Continued To the Session in may next
and m^r Parsons Consenting thereto The Same is accordingly Continued under view that in the mean time the matter may be accomodated

this Court is adjourned to the 2^d Tuesday in march next to sitt
[in] Worcester, at ye house of Daniell Haywood

---

[1] The title of *Clerk* was formerly given to a clergyman or any educated
person.

WORCESTER ss *Anno Regni Regis Georgij Secundi Magnæ Brittaniæ Franciæ Hiberniæ Quinto*

Att a Court of General Sessions of the peace held at Worcester for & within the County of Worcester the Second Tuesday of March being the 14ᵗʰ day of Said Month Anno Domʸ 1731-2 by adjournment from the 1ˢᵗ Tuesday of February last past

———

Benjamin Townsend of Worcester in said County Husbandman being bound over to this Court by mʳ Justice Jenison to answer to such matters and things as shall be objected against him on his majestys behalf and Especially for the abuse he offered at a Court held before the said William Jenison Esq the 22ⁿᵈ day of February last past at the house of Thomas Starnes in Worcester in said County Inholder which Court was held by virtue of a speciall warrant, and the said Townsend to be of the good behaviour in the mean time towards his majesty and all his Leige people &c the said Benjamin Townsend came into Court and to the matters alledged against him pleaded not Guilty and putt himself on Tryal by a Jury whereupon the Court Order that the Case be Continued to the next Court of Generall Sessions of the peace to be holden at Worcester aforesaid on the Second Tuesday of May next and that the said Benjamin Townsend give bond with two Suretys for his appearance at said Court and abideing Judgment &c and In the mean time to be of the good behaviour towards his majestye

6

and all his Leige people, The said Benjamin Townsend Recognized as principall In the Sum of Thirty pounds & Thomas Hapgood and Jotham Rice as Suretys in fifteen pounds Each ; for the said Benjamin Townsends appearance & abiding the Judgment of said Court & being of ye good behaviour in ye mean time &c̈t

The above Recognizance was Discharged may 1732

Sarah Read of Rutland In the County aforesaid Housewife & wife of Thomas Read of said Rutland being bound over by way of Recognizance to the Court of Generall Sessions of the peace In February last past by m^r Justice Wright to answer for the Sin of fornication &c̈t and being not able to Travell to said Court her bonds were Continued to this time She now appeared in Court and Pleaded Guilty where upon the Court order that for her Crime she pay a fine of three pounds or be whiped on the Naked back five Stripes & pay the Cost of her prosecution and stand Committed till Sentence be Performed, Cost Taxed at one pound six shillings & six pence, She paid the fine & Cost in Court which was Divid to the Justices present in part of what is due to them being 8/7 apeice

---

The Town of Worcester being presented by the Grand Jurors of said County for their not being provided with Stocks as the law Directs at this Court in February last past appeared before this Court by their Selectmen and pleaded Guilty to the presentment, and makeing it appear that they have now a good and lawfull pair of Stocks and praying the Courts favour Its ordered that the said Town be Discharged from paying a fine for said Defect & that they pay Cost Taxed at one pound Eight Shillings & Sixpence

ye Cost is paid

The Committee appointed by this Court in February last past for the building a Goal &c̈t laid before them an acc^{ott} of their proceedings which was approved on

The Severall accompts following were laid before the Court and were allowed and payment ordered to be made to Discharge them out of the County Treasury vizt

an accott of John Chandler Jun Esq amounting unto Twenty Three pounds Ten Shillings & nine pence	23 10 9
an accott of William Jenison Esq of one pound fifteen Shillings & six pence	1 15 6
an accott of Henry Lee Esq one pound ten shillings & three pence	1 10 3
an accot of Richard Wheeler & others of four pounds five shillings	4 5
an accott of Robert Barber of one pound Ten shillings & nine pence	1 10 9
Amounting in the whole to Thirty two pounds Twelve Shillings & 3 pence	32 12 3

And the Clerk is accordingly ordered To Signifie the Same to the County Treasurer.

also To Phinehas Hayward 20/ for Irons for the Cage

And the Court was adjourned without day

NOTES.

THE FIRST JAIL. (page 35) The first Jail proper, which was not completed until 1733, was on the present Lincoln Street, a short distance from Lincoln Square. The house of Judge Jennison, where the prisoners were kept for a time, was on the site of State Street, about half-way up the hill. Daniel Heywood lived where the Bay State House now is, corner of Main and Exchange Streets.

STOCKS, WEIGHTS AND MEASURES. (page 35) Each town was to be provided with Stocks and a full set of weights and measures under the penalty of fines for non-compliance.

SCHOOLMASTER. (page 35) The penalty for neglecting or refusing to maintain a school a certain number of months in the year, was thirty pounds for every town of 150 families, forty pounds for 200 families, and so *pro rata.*

PUNISHMENT FOR FORNICATION. (page 36)   Fornication was punishable by a fine not to exceed five pounds or whipping on the naked body not to exceed "ten stripes apiece."   The offence of adultery appears to have been ignored by this Court, married and single alike being tried for fornication.

NEGLECT TO ATTEND PUBLIC WORSHIP. (page 36)   "And be it . . enacted, That if any Person being able of Body and not otherwise necessarily prevented, shall for the space of one Month together absent themselves from the publick Worship of God on the Lord's-Day, they shall forfeit and pay the Sum of *ten Shillings.*

"*Provided* always. That if upon Trial it shall appear that any Person so charged, had good and sufficient Excuse for their Absence, such Person shall be dismissed without Costs."

It will be observed in the foregoing cases that the persons tried, while declared innocent, were ordered to pay costs, notwithstanding the law expressly provided for exemption in such cases.   Numerous other instances of this method of dispensing justice will be found in the records of this Court. In the matter of leaving his cash behind, the guilt or innocence of the culprit made little difference.   This sagacity is ofttimes emulated in our modern courts.

ANABAPTISTS. (page 38)   Anabaptists and Quakers were exempted from paying the general ministerial tax.   The law required that a list of the names of such persons in each town should be presented to the Court.

WORCESTER ss *Anno Regni Regis Georgij Secundi nunc Magniæ Brittaniæ Franciæ Et Hiberniæ Quinto* ⌒

Att a Court of General Sessions of yᵉ peace Holden at Worcester for and within the County of Worcester the Second Tuesday of May being the Ninth day of Said Month Annoq Dominij 1732

JUSTICES PRESENT

JOHN CHANDLER	⎤ Esqrs ⎬ Justices of ⎦ the Peace & Quorum	SAMUELL WRIGHT	⎤
JOSEPH WILDER		JOSIAH WILLARD	⎬ Esqrˢ
WILLIAM WARD		JOSEPH DWIGHT	⎥ Justices
WILLIAM JENISON		SAMUEL DUDLEY	⎥
DANIEL TAFT	⎱ Esqrs ⎰ Justices	HENRY LEE	⎥
JOHN CHANDLER Junʳ		NAHUM WARD	⎦

———

Names of yᵉ Grand Jurors who served this year

Mʳ Thomas Rice Foreman	Mʳ Gershom Rice
Mʳ Ebenʳ Wilder	Mʳ Josiph Baron
Mʳ James Keith	Mʳ Joseph Banister
Mʳ Isaac Learned	Mʳ Parcivall Hall
Mʳ Daniell Denney	Mʳ John Woods
Mʳ Daniell How	Mʳ Joseph Stevens
Mʳ Robert Taft	Mʳ Edward Hartwell

Served 2 days

The names of the Grand Jurers who were Returned to Serve the present year vizt.

Oxford Cap' Ebenezer Learned   Worcester M' James Taylor
                foreman
Lancaster M' John Bennitt   Mendon M' Ebenezer Daniells
Woodstock M' Ephraim Child   Brookfield M' Samuell Barnes
Westborough M' Isaac Tomlin   Sutton M' Nathanael Dyke
Leicester M' Thomas Richardson   Southborough M' Samuel Ward
Rutland M' Edward Rice   Shrewsbury M' John Crosby
Uxbridge M' Woodland Thompson
                                 Lunenburg M' Ephraim Peirce

who were Sworn & the Charge being given them were Dismist Till The next Term.   Each attended one day :

Constables that attended were Robert Peibles 2 days James Calwell 4 days

---

The Court proceeded To sort ye Votes for ye Choice of a County Treasurer, And M' Jonathan Houghton of Lancaster was Chose by a major Vote & was Sworn accordingly

---

The acco' of ye Charge of ye Grandjurors That Served at ye Court of Assize & Generall Goal Delivery in September last amounting unto thirteen pounds thirteen Shillings was Examined & allowed and payment ordered thereupon accordingly for   13 13

also ye acc' of ye Grandjurors that Served at ye Court from august last amounting unto forty nine pounds Seventeen Shillings was accordingly allow'd & paym' ordered for   49 19

The order given accordingly   Totall   63 12

The Towns following being presented by ye Grandjurors for Sundry Defects appeared by their Respective Selectmen, and were Excused paying Costs   viz'

Southborough three presentments—Uxbridge two presentments —Brookfield one presentment—Lunenburg one presentment— Rutland one presentment—and Cost were paid accordingly

---

The Committee appointed for building ye Goal &c^t laid before ye Court an acco^t of their proceedings which were approved and thereupon the Court ordered that the County Treasurer pay to ye Committee or their order the Sum of one hundred pounds by the last day of May next & the further Sum of Seventy pounds by the last day of July next To Enable them To pay the Two first payments they are obliged To towards building the Said Goal &c^t

---

Upon Reading the Petition of the Reverend Mr David Parsons of Leicester in behalf of himself & family Seting forth that the Petitioner accepted the Call of the Church and Town of Leicester, to the Gospell ministry among them Sometime in the year 1721 with an Incouragement from them of an Honourable Support of Seventy five pounds &c^t from year to year in which Service the Petitioner has Continued ever since according To his poor Capacity heartily Endeavoured to be faithfull. But the Town has been formerly very negligent in Supporting of him and his family which has necesitated him to many Long and Grevious processes at ye Session in Middlesex for the Same where he Recovered Judgment against them at least for a part till ye year 1730, which began with march Since which they have been wholly Deficient in Every part which has put him to Distressing Difficultys to Support himself & Carry on his Work &c^t praying the Court would take his Case into their Serious Consideration and in their Wisdom and Justice according to the Direction of the good laws of this province take Effectual Care for the Support of the Petitioner & his family by causing the Town of Leicester Imediately To pay in a Sutable Consideration for the Petitioners Service in the Gospell ministry amongst them for ye year 1730 & otherwise to find Such further or other Reliefe in the premises as the Court Shall think fitt to Inable the Petitioner in his duty for yᵉ future &cᵗ as by the Petition on file. The Selectmen of Leicester being Summoned by a warrant from this Court to make answer to this Petition at the Court of Generall Sessions of the peace held at this place on the first Tuesday of February last past, appearing Desired this Case might be Continued To this time under a view that the matter might be accomodated to which mʳ Parsons Consented and now the Sᵈ Selectmen appeared vizt Richard Southgate Daniell Denney Thomas Newhall Thomas Richardson & Samuel Green and acknowledged the Town of Leicesters Contract with the Revᵈ mʳ Parsons and that his yearly Sallary was Seventy five pounds a year and that the Town had been negligent in not Supporting Said mʳ Parsons. The Court having therefore Duly Considered the Case are of opinion that they are Guilty and order that the said mesʳˢ Richard Southgate Daniel Denney Thomas Newhall Thomas Richardson and Samuel Green the said Selectmen be fined the Sum of four pounds each according to The direction of the law in that Case made and provided for that it appears to be a Second neglect of the maintainance of their minister, and to pay Costs of prosecution Taxed at Three pounds nine shillings & Six pence, and Samuel Wright Esq Messʳˢ Benjamin Flagg Jun. of Worcester & mʳ Jonas Houghton of Lancaster be assessors, to assess and apportion the Sum of Seventy five pounds upon the Inhabitants of Said Town of Leicester in Such manner as is Directed for raising other Publick Charges and to present Such assessment unto Two Justices of the peace Quorum Unus that so a Warrant may be affixed thereto for the leveying and Collecting the Same according to the laws of this province and upon Such Collection to pay the Same to Henry Lee Esq of Worcester who is appointed by this Court To Receive and pay the Same to the Revᵈ mʳ David Parsons for his Sallary for the year 1730, begining with march

The Selectmen of Leicester appealed from the Judgment of this Court to the next Court of assize and General Goal Delivery to be holden at Worcester within and for the County of Worcester. on the Wednesday Imediately preceeding The time by law appointed for holding Said Court of assize & Generall Goal Delivery at Springfield in and for the County of Hampshire in September next and Entered into Recognizance pursuant to law to prosecute their appeal as aforesaid with Effect.

Richard Southgate of Leicester In the County of Suffolk Husbandman as principal In the Sum of Twenty pounds & Daniell Denney and Thomas Newhall as Suretys in Ten pounds Each acknowledged themselves to be Indebted to m^r David Parsons of Leicester Clark to be Leveyed on their Severall goods or Chattells Lands or Tenaments and in want thereof on their bodys for the use of the said David Parsons Conditioned that the said Selectmen of the Town of Leicester shall prosecute their appeal as aforesaid with Effect

Attes^t John Chandler J^r Cler pea

The Court was adjourned without day

7

WORCESTER ss   *Anno R R' Georgij Secundi nunc Magniæ Brittaniæ Franciæ Et Hiberniæ Sexto*

At a Court of Generall Sessions of the peace held at Worcester for and within the County of Worcester on the Second Tuesday of Augst Being the Eighth day of Said Month, Anno Dom; 1732

JUSTICES PRESENT WERE

JOHN CHANDLER Esq ⎫ Justices of
JOSEPH WILDER Esq ⎪
WILLIAM WARD Esq ⎬ the Peace
WILLIAM JENISON Esq ⎭ & Quorum

DANIEL TAFT Esq
JOHN CHANDLER J Esq

SAMUELL WRIGHT Esq
JOSIAH WILLARD Esq
JOSEPH DWIGHT Esq
SAMUEL DUDLEY Esq
HENRY LEE Esq
NAHUM WARD Esq

————

Names of the Grandjurors that attended

Capt Ebenezer Learned foreman
Mr James Taylor
Mr James Holden
Mr John Bennitt
Mr Jonas Houghton
Mr Nath^{ll} Dyke
Mr Ephraim Childs
Mr Isaac Tomlin

Mr Thomas Richardson
Mr Samuel Ward
Mr John Crosby
Mr Woodland Thompson
Mr Ephraim Peirce
Served 2 days each and Mr John Eddy Constable of Oxford attended them

A Petition or Complaint of Daniel Taft of Mendon In ye County of Worcester Esq—Shewing that there being no Publick highway or Countey Road Leading from Worcester To Mendon whereby persons who have (Since ye Erecting a County) dayly business To Transact in the Shire Town &ct are greatly damaged &ct humbly moving to the Court that they would Conformable to Law order a Committee to view the lands in and between Said Towns &ct and make Report to this Court at their next Session, or at this present Session in Case that it Should be adjourned that the Court may act thereon as by the Petition on file will appear Read and the Court appoint Wm Jenison Daniell Taft & Sam^{ll} Dudley Esqrs a Committee To view The lands in & between ye Towns of Worcester & Mendon and make Report as Soon as may be what may bee what may be proper for the Court To act concerning ye premises

————

A List of the Presentments made by the Grand Jurors to this Court vizt The Grandjurers for ye body of the County of Worcester upon their Oaths do present Margaret Newton of Southborough in the Said County Spinstress for her being Guilty of Fornication and do Likewise present ye Town of Shrewsbury for their not being provided with a writing & Reading Schoolmaster as ye law Requires which things are against the good and wholesome laws of this province and ye peace of our Sovereign Lord the King his Crown & Dignity   Joseph Dwight attor pro. Rego :

Billa vera   Ebenezer Learned foreman

————

A memoriall of Eleazur Fletcher of Sutton Showing that the m[em]orialist lives Six miles distance from the meeting house in Sutton & that about Two miles thereof there is no Road or way laid out and that he with Others his neighbours are necessatated to Trespass on other mens lands to go to meeting & having adrest ye Select men of Sutton for Reliefe are Refused any, praying this Court would be pleased to Redress the great Difficulty he with others at present Labour under as by the memorial on file will appear the Court Order that the Selectmen of Sutton be Cited to appear before this Court on Wednesday ye 20th of Sepr next at two aclock afternoon To make answer to ye above memoriall or Complaint & Shew Cause if any they have why the prayer of [the petitioners] Should not be granted

---

David Parsons of Leicester In the County of Worcester Clr versus The Select men of Leicester &ct as by the Sumons will appear
The partys appeared in Court & desired the Case might be Continued till The next Term and it accordingly was.

Samuel Gibs and Lydiah his wife and Hezekiah Moore were bound over by way of Recognizance by Joseph Wilder Esq To appear at the Court of Generall Sessions of ye peace held in may last, to answer Severally for the Sin of fornication their Recognizances were Continued to this Court, and the persons now all appeared & Pleaded Guilty The Court thereupon order that they pay each a fine of thirty Shillings & Cost of Suit, or be whiped on the naked body five Stripes Each which was done in Court & they were discharged

---

Jonathan Newton & Tabitha his wife were bound over by way of Recognizance by Wm Ward Esq to appear at this Court to answer for the Sin of fornication Committed by them before mariage the partys appeared & pleaded Guilty The Court thereupon order that they each pay a fine of thirty Shillings & Cost of Court or be whipt on ye naked body five Stripes each & stand Committed till Sentance be performed   Judgment Satisfied in Court

---

The Towns of Brookfield and Lunenburg be[ing] presented by the Grandjurors for not being duly provided with a Standard of

weights and measures as the law Requires appeared by their Selectmen and being now provided therewith were Excused paying
Costs

———

Samuell Leightle & Mary Warden being Bound over to this
Court by way of Recognizance by Joseph Dwight Esq to appear
at this Court To answer for their presuming to Lye together in one
and the same bed being both undress'd appeared in Court &
pleaded Guilty The Court thereupon order that they pay as a
fine for their offence Twenty Shillings each & Costs which was
done in Court

———

The Court now order that a Sutable and Convenient Court house
be built on the land Given by Wᵐ Jenison Esqr for that Purpose,
and Wᵐ Jenison John Chandler Jun & Henry Lee Esqrs or any
Two of them are appointed a Committee In the Name of this Court
to Inform the Gent at Boston or Elsewhere who have an Interest in
land (in yᵉ County and Especially) in yᵉ Town of Worcester and
by that Towns being made the Shire Town are greatly advanced
of the Courts Intention & to Know what any of them will be
pleased to give towards building & adorning Said house and Said
Committee are desired to wait upon said Gents and with them to
advise what manner of a House to build, and to make Report to
this Court thereof and of what it may Cost as soon as may bee that
So the Court may the better Know what measures to take Respecting the affair

[A copy of this record was given to Henry Lee indorsed as follows:

To Henry Lee Esq

Sr   We desire you to act in our Names
Concerning the within mentioned premises as fully as if either or both of us
were in Boston

yr friends & Servts

WILLIAM JENISON
JOHN CHANDLER Jr]

The Court Order that the Committee appointed for building the
Prison &ᶜᵗ make Such additions thereto as they may judge most
proper and Especially to Enlarge the yard

An acco" of Daniell Gookin Esqr Sheriff of the County presented
for payment Read & ordered that the Hon" Joseph Wilder Esqʳ
& Henry Lee Esqr be a Committee to auditt & Examin the Same
and Report what may be proper for the Court to do thereon at
the adjournment in September next

In as much as the Prison or Goal is in a great measure finished
It is ordered by the Court that the Cage in the Chamber of yᵉ
house of mʳ Dan" Heywood be forthwith Taken down. but that
the house remain a Goal (Still for Such persons as give bond for
the Liberty of the Yard &ᶜᵗ) Till the further order of this Court
together with the new Goal, and as occasion may be the Sheriff is
directed and Impowered to Remove such prisoners as are or may
be under his Care as Goal Keeper To and from either Goal for
their more Safe Keeping

A Petition of the Select men of Brookfield shewing that one
Hinds an ancient woman and an Inhabitant of Said Town having
no means to Support her self has of late become a Town Charge.
but that they apprehend her children or some of them ought by
law to be Charged with her maintanance praying the Court would
take yᵉ premises into Consideration so that what to Justice doth
appertain may be done as by the Petition on file &ᶜᵗ—Read &
being duly Considered ordered that the Children of yᵉ said
Hinds be Cited to appear before the Court of Generall Sessions of
yᵉ peace to be held at Worcester on the first Tuesday of November next To shew Cause if any they have why they should not be
assessed according to law for the maintainance of their said
mother

William King & Benj^a Marsh Returned a list of ye Ana Baptists in Sutton according to the Courts order of Feb^r last past—and under oaths thereto

Thomas Green and Daniell Denney Returned a List of the ana baptists in Leicester according to ye Courts order of Feb : last past & made oaths thereto

Then the Court adjourned to Wednesday ye 20 of Sepr next to this place 2 "Clock P : m—·

WORCESTER ss *Anno Regni Regis Georgij Secundi nunc Magniæ Brittaniæ Franciæ et Hiberniæ Sexto*

At a Court of Generall Sessions of the Peace held (by adjournment from ye Second Tuesday of Aug^st last past) at Worcester for and within the County of Worcester on Sept. 20. 1732

William Jenison Daniell Taft & Samuel Dudley Esq^rs a Committee appointed by this Court to view the lands in and between the Towns of Mendon & Worcester in answer to a Petition of Danl Taaft Esq in order for a Publick highway or Countey Roads being laid out &c^t made Report as on file and accepted ; The said Committee laid before the Court an acco^t of their Charge amounting unto the Sum of Seven pounds one Shilling & Ten pence which was also approved of by the Court,—And

This Court order the Clerk in their name to make out a warrant Directed To the Sheriff or his Deputy To Sumons a Jury of Good and lawfull men Quallyfyed according to law to meet at the Dwelling House of Mr William Rawson in Mendon in said County on monday the Second day of October next who after they have had an oath duly administered To them by a Justice of the peace lay out the way above Refered to according to the best of their Skill and Judgment pursuant to law having a due Regard to the Report of the Com^tee the Said Sheriff or his Deputy To make due Return of their doings to this Court at their next Court of Gen^ll Sessions in November next as well under his own as the hands of the Jurors by whose oaths the Same is laid out.

At a Court of Generall Sessions of y⁰ peace held at Worcester in & for the County of Worcester the first Tuesday of November being the 7th day of Said month annoq Dom. 1732

John Chandler Esq Joseph Wilder Esq Wm Ward Esq Wm Jenison Esq Jus^t : pac : & Quo.

John Chandler J^r Joseph Dwight Samuel Dudley Henry Lee & Nahum Ward Esqr Jus : pac

The whole Grandjury attended one day & Wm Calwell attended them

---

The presentments of ye Towns of Sutton were read and Said Towns were excused paying Cost

---

David Parsons of Leicester In ye County of Worcester Cler pla^t versus the Selectmen of ye Town of Leicester Def^t &c̃t as ᵱ ye Sumons will appear ; the partys apeared in Court and ye action at ye desire of ye said Selectmen Mr Parsons Consenting was Continued To ye next Term in Febry

8

John Sibly of Sutton & his wife John Stebings of Leicester & his
wife abner Newton Southboro' and his wife being Severally bound
over to this Court to answer for ye Sin of fornication Severally
pleaded Guilty & were fined thirty Shillings each and payd Costs
& were dismist

Mr Sheriff Gookin withdrew his former acco^{tt} and at this Court
Exhibitted a new acco^{tt} was comitted to Joseph Wilder & Henry
Lee Esq^s to auditt Examin & Report on ye Same to ye Court in
Febry next

The Court desire [and] order that the Sheriff at ye Charge of
ye County provide Two Course Straw beds & Two Straw bolsters
& four blanketts for ye use of such prisoners as are now or may
hereafter be in his majestys Goal in this County and lay his acco^t
before ye Court for payment

The Court order that for ye present and untill the further order
of this Court that the prison be ye House of Correction and y^t y^e
Goal Keeper be the master of said House of Correction attending
to ye Directions of ye Law in Such Case made and provided

. The Court order that William Jenison John Chandler Henry
Lee Esqs & m^r Benjamin fflag Junr be a Comittee for Seeing y^e
Court house built & finished which the Court have agreed To
build, & the said house not to Exceed Thirty six feet Long Twenty
six feet wide & thirteen feet post, & to be done after their best
Judgment & discretion either by hiring men or leting the Same
out by the Great & Report what they Doe to ye Court in February
next

The Court order that there be a County Tax or assessment amounting to ye Sum of Three hundred & Eleven pounds one Shilling & fourpence Raised on the Severall Towns within the County according to the Directions of the law for defraying the usuall necessary Charges of ye County & for building a Court house and that the Clerk of the Court forthwith Send out warrants to the Selectmen or assessors of the Respective Towns for assessing ye Severall Towns proportion thereof as ye law directs & for paying in ye Same to m^r Jonathan Houghton County Treasurer his Successor or his order at or before ye last day of may next Insuing

The Severall Towns Proportion are as follows vizt

Worcester	Twenty Two pounds fifteen Shillings & 4d	22	15	4
Lancaster	Sixty Two pounds Sixteen Shillings & 8d	62	16	8
Mendon	Thirty Six pounds	36		
Woodstock	Thirty Two pounds	32		
Brookfield	Twenty Seven pounds one Shilling & 4d	27	1	4
Southboro'	Seventeen pounds Six Shillings	17	6	
Leicester	thirteen pounds nineteen Shillings & 4d	13	19	4
Rutland	Seven pounds Sixteen Shillings	7	16	
Westboro'	Eighteen pounds Two Shillings	18	2	
Shrewsbury	fourteen pounds fourteen Shillings	14	14	
Oxford	fourteen pounds four Shillings	14	4	
Sutton	Twenty four pounds Ten Shillings	24	10	
Uxbridge	Twelve pounds & 8d	12	0	8
Lunenburg	Seven pounds Sixteen Shillings	7	16	
	Sum Total	£311	1	4

Warrants were accordingly Issued out Novr 14: 1732

Att John Chandler J^r Cler pac

The Town of Lunenburg having Chosen Mr Isaac Farnsworth Sealer for weights & measures he was according[ly] Sworn in Court   att John Chandler J^r Cle pac

This Witnesseth That I James Buttler of Lancaster in ye County of Worcester husbandman do hereby fully freely and absolutely

Release acquit & Discharge John Hind Hopestill Hinds and Enoch
Hinds all of Brookfield & Jacob Hinds of Shrewsbury all in Said
County of Worcester and province of ye Massachusetts Bay in
New England from all & any manner of Payments Charge or Expence for or towards the maintainance Subsistance or Support of
Mary Hinds ye naturall mother of ye aforesaid Hinds vizt John
Hopestill Jacob & Enoch Hinds as afors^d and do hereby under-
take and engage to maintain and Support ye Said Mary Hinds
dure[ing] her naturall life in Comfortable and Decent manner and
for me my heirs Ex^{rs} & adm^{rs} do promise and engage to free Discharge the Said John Hopestill Jacob & Enoch Hinds aforesaid
from any manner of Charge or expence for the Support or maintainance of the said Mary Hinds during her natural life as aforesaid   in Witness whereof I do hereunto Sett my hand ye 8th day
of febry 1732/33   his
      witness   James X Buttler
Richard Wilds   mark
Howard Southgate

Worcester ss Worcester Feb^r 8th : 1732/3   James Butler
within named personally appearing freely acknowledged this In-
stm^t to be his act & Deed   Before me   John Chandler J^r Jus pac

   Entered from ye originall Rec^d Feb^r 8th 1732/3
                     ℔   John Chandler J^r Cla pac

WORCESTER ss   *Anno R^i R^s Georgij Secundi nunc Magnæ Britaniæ Franciæ et Hiberniæ Sexto*

At *His Majestys* Court of Generall Sessions of the Peace begun and Held at Worcester in and for the County of Worcester on the first Tuesday of February being the Sixth day of Said month Anno Dom : 1732-3

JUSTICES PRESENT

John Chandler Esq Joseph Wilder Esq Wm Ward Esq Wm Jenison Esq Jus of ye Pac & Qurum

John Chandler J^r Samuel Wright Joseph Dwight Saml Dudley Henry Lee & Nahum Ward Esq^s Justices of ye Peace.

Names of ye Grandjury that attended this Court

Capt Ebenezer Learned foreman	Mr James Holden
Mr John Bennett	Mr Ephraim Child
Mr Isaac Tomlin	Mr Thomas Richardson
Mr Edward Rice	Capt Jonas Houghton
Mr James Taylor	Mr Saml Barns
Mr Eleazur Daniells	Mr Saml Ward
Mr Nathan^l Dyke	each attended two days and W^m
Mr Woodland Thompson	Colwell Constable attended on them

———

Ralph Hill of Mendon & Hannah his wife being heretofore presented by the Grandjurors for being Guilty of ye Crime of fornication before marriage & being Recognized To appear at this Court now appeared & pleaded Guilty, were find Each fifty Shillings To our Sovereign Lord the King & Cost wch they paid & were dismiss'd

————

Margarett Newton of Southboro' appeared before ye Court & pleaded Guilty to her presentment for the Crime of fornication, was fin'd to our Lord ye King in ye Sum of thirty Shillings & Cost, She paid ye fine and was Dismiss'd, ye Cost given to her

————

John Ellis of Uxbridge appeared before ye Court and Complained of himself for being Guilty of ye Crime of fornication with Han^a his wife before marriage, was find to our Lord ye King &c̄t ye Sum of thirty Shillings & to pay Costs which he paid and was Dismiss'd

————

Personally appeared before ye Court John Ellis of Uxbridge in S^d County Husbandman and John Harwood of Said Uxbridge Retailer & acknowledged themselves bound to our Sovereign Lord the King, &c̄t vizt The Said John Ellis as Principall In the Sum of Ten pounds & ye said John Harwood as Surety in ye Sum of Ten pounds &c̄t Conditioned that if Hannah Ellis wife of the said John Ellis shall appear before the next Court of Gen^{ll} Sessions of ye peace to be held here on the Second Tuesday of may next to answer to her being Guilty of the Crime of fornication Then ye Recog' to be void Else to Remain in full force & virtue

————

George Wicker Servant of   Baldwin now living in Leicester in this County having absented himself from his Said masters Service and ye Charge of pursuing and Recovering him amounting to eight pounds Sixteen Shillings and the Said George being before

ye Court and acknowledgeing ye Same the Court therefore order
that the Said apprentice Serve his Said master his heirs Excut^r or
adm^rs eight months next after the determination of ye present In-
denture

———

Obadiah Coolige of Marlborough in ye County of Midlesex
Cordwainer who was bound by way of Recognizance by Nahum
Ward Esqr one of his Majestys Justices of the peace for ye County
of Worcester To appear before ye Justices of our Lord ye King at
the Court of Generall Sessions of the peace held at Worcester &c^t
on ye first Tuesday of Novr. last past to answer to Such matters
and things as Should be Objected against him on his maj^tys behalf
and Especially to answer To a Complaint made against him before
S^d Justice for theifishly Taking a fourty shilling bill out of ye house
of Simon Maynard in Shrewsbury on or about ye 21st day of aprill
1732 &c^t as by ye Recognizance will appear having faild of appearing said Recognizance was by the Said Court then declared forfieted ; but he now appearing and producing Testimony Sufficient
that he was under such bodily Indisposition as Rendered him unable of attending at ye Court praying the forficture of ye Recog' :
may be Remitted, for that Reason that he might be admitted to a
Tryall The Court thereupon order that upon his Entering into a
new Recognizance with Two Sufficient Suretys vizt The said Obadiah Coolidge as principall In ye Sum of Twenty pounds & his
Suretys In Ten pounds Each To appear at the next Court of Gen^ll
Sessions of the peace To be held at this place on the Second
Tuesday of may next To answer To ye aforesaid Complaint &c^t
that said forficture of said Recognizance be Remitted, and further
ordered that Symon Maynard the Complainant Enter into Recognizance with Surutys as well To our Sovereign Lord the King to
prosecute his Complaint ag^st ye Said obadiah Coolidge, as also to
ye said obadiah Coolidge To answer all Damages in Case he Dont
Supporte his Complaint. The said Maynard accordingly Recognized himself as principall in Twenty pounds Each Recognizance
& Gershom Rice yeoman & Benj^a fflagg Junr Gent both of Wor-

cester in said County as Suretys in Ten pounds each in Each Recognizance ; but the said Coolidge faild of Renewing his Recognizance

———

Daniel Gookin Esqr Sheriff of yᵉ County pursuant to a warrant Issued by the Clerk by order of this Court having Impanelled a Jury & Laid out or Bounded yᵉ Road from mendon to Worcester made Report at the last Court of Generall Sessions of the peace held here in Novʳ last—as also an accoᵗ of the Charge thereof which was Refered to this Court, & the Court now order that the further Consideration thereof be Refered To yᵉ Second Tuesday of May next ;

———

A Petition of yᵉ Town of Sutton and also a Petition of Sundry of the Inhabitants of Hassanamisco praying the Road lately laid out by order of this Court Leading from Worcester to Mendon may not be Confirmed but that it may be laid out thro' Hassanamisco for Reason In Said Petitions mentioned   Read & ordered that The Petitioners Serve the Town of Mendon and Uxbridge with Copys of Said Petitions that they Shew Cause if any they have at yᵉ next Court of Generall Sessions of yᵉ peace to be holden at Worcester on the Second Tuesday of May next why the Prayer of Said Petitions should not be answer'd

———

A Petition of John Harwood in behalf of the Town of Uxbridge Returning the thanks of said Town to the Court for yᵉ Road lately laid out from Mendon to Worcester & praying they may have a Road laid out from Uxbridge to meet with the aforesaid Road &cᵗ Read and Refered to the Second Tuesday of May next for further Consideration

———

An accoⁿ of yᵉ Grand Jurers that attended on his Majestys Court of assize and Genⁱⁱ Goal Delivery begun and held at Worcester yᵉ third Wednesday in Septem' anno Dom' 1732 present for allowance amounting To 14¹ 4ˢ/ Read & Examined and The Treasurer of the County is hereby ordered to pay the Same to yᵉ persons to whome the same is Respectively due or to their orders in full discharge thereof

———

An acco' of John Chandler Jun' amounting to Six pounds was presented for allowance   Read & ordered that the Treasurer of the County pay the Sum of Six pounds to the accompttant in full Discharge thereof

———

Joseph Wilder Esqr from yᵉ Committee appointed the 7ᵗʰ of Nov' 1732 to Examine the acco' of Daniel Gookin Esq Sheriff of this County made Report thereon which was Read & accepted & thereupon The Court Order that the Treas' of the County to pay To yᵉ Said Daniell Gookin Esq fifteen pounds Twelve Shillings in full Discharge thereof

———

The presentment of the Grandjurors To this Court is as follows

Att a Court of Generall Sessions of yᵉ peace holden at Worcester within and for yᵉ County of Worcester on Tuesday yᵉ 6ᵗʰ day of febry anno Dominij 1732/3   The Grand Jury for yᵉ body of yᵉ Said County upon their oaths do present Peter Corlile of Leicester within yᵉ said County Husbandman for prophane Swearing[1] on Tuesday yᵉ 30ᵗʰ day of January last and also for uttering many menaces and threatning Speeches ag'ᵗ Thomas Richardson of Leicester aforesaid Inholder, and also do present James Nuting Husbandman Josiah Nuting Husbandman and John Nuting Husbandman all of Hassanamisco in yᵉ Said County each and all of them for Travelling Unnecessarily on yᵉ Saturday evening after Sun sett before yᵉ Lords Day[2] from Lancaster to Groton—also Philip Chase of ———— within the said County of Worcester for Labouring unnecessarily on ye Lords day, as also Elisha Johnson of Sutton in the County aforesaid Gent for not building & keeping in Repair two bridges on the Two Branches of Black Stones River in ye bounds of Hassanamisco as by his own Covenant and by law he ought all and every of which things are against the peace of our Lord the King his Crown and Dignity and the good and wholsome laws of this Gov[t] Joseph Dwight attorney pro Rego

Eben[r] Learned foreman

Entered ℘ John Chandler J[r] Cle pac

This Court order, The Clerk in the name of the Court To Return their thanks to m[r] Jonas Clark of Boston Brazier for the Coat of arms he has made the County a present off and for the Constables Stafs ;

Then the Court was adjourned without day

Att[s] John Chandler J[r] Cle pac

NOTES.

The laws against profanity and sabbath-breaking in force at this date were as follows: (See page 65.)

SWEARING.—"Be it enacted" etc. "That if any Person or Persons shall prophanely Swear or Curse in the hearing of any Justice of the Peace, or shall be thereof convicted by the Oaths of two Witnesses, or Confession of the Party, before any Justice or Justices of the Peace: Every such Offender shall forfeit and pay into the Use of the Poor of the Town, where the Offence shall be committed, the Sum of *five Shillings*. And if the Offender be not able to pay the said Sum, then to be set in the Stocks, not exceeding two Hours. And if any Person shall utter more profane Oaths or Curses at the same time, and hearing of the same Person or Persons, he shall forfeit and pay to the Use aforesaid, the Sum of *twelve Pence* for every Oath or Curse after the first; or be set in the Stocks three Hours.

"*Provided*, That every Offence against this Law shall be complained of and proved as aforesaid, within thirty Days next after the Offence committed."

SABBATH BREAKING.—"Be it enacted That all Persons who shall be found in the Streets, Wharffs, Fields, or other Places within any Town on the Evening following the Lord's Day, disporting, playing making a Disturbance, or committing any Rudeness: The Persons so offending, shall each of them pay a Fine of *five Shillings*, or suffer twelve Hours Imprisonment, or sit in the Stocks, not exceeding two Hours. All Fines and Forfeitures arising by Virtue of this Act, ... shall be to and for the Use of the Poor of the Town where the Offence shall be committed," etc.

"And the Constables of the respective Towns are hereby directed and specially impowered to prevent the Prophanation of the Lord's Day, by restraining Persons from walking, recreating and disporting themselves in the Streets, Wharffs, or Fields, in the Time of publick Worship."

In the olden time in New England the Sabbath began at sunset on Saturday and ended at the same time on Sunday.

WORCESTER ss   *Anno R^i R^a Georgij Secundi nunc Magnæ Brittainiæ Franciæ et Hiberniæ Sexto*

Att his majestys Court of Generall Sessions of the Peace Held at Worcester in and for ye County of Worcester on the Second Tuesday of May being ye 8th day of Said month Anno Dom. 1733

John Chandler Esq Joseph Wilder Esq Wm Ward Esq Wm Jenison Esq Justices of ye peace & Quorum

Daniel Taft John Chandler Samuell Wright Joseph Dwight Samuel Dudley Henry Lee &Nahum Ward Esq^{rs} Justices of ye peace

---

Grand Jurors that attended this Court

Capt Ebenezer Learned foreman	Mr Thomas Richardson
Capt Jonas Houghton	Mr John Crosby
Mr Ephraim Child	Mr James Holden
Mr Nathanael Dyke	Mr Eleazer Daniells
Mr Edward Rice	Mr Isaac Tomlin
Mr Ephraim Peirce	Mr Samuel Ward
Mr James Taylor	Mr Woodland Thompson
Mr John Benett	
Mr Samuel Barns	

The names of ye Gent Returned to Serve on ye Grandjury for the Current year

Mr Gershom Rice foreman	Mr Moses How
Mr Hooker Osgood	Mr Samuel Johnson
Mr Wm Old	Mr James Moore
Mr Wm Brown	Mr Thomas Thayer
Capt Richard Moore	Mr David Maynard
Mr Richard Davenport	Mr Edward Morris
Mr Jonathan Farnsworth	Mr Samuel Lillie
Mr Wm Richardson	Mr James Newton
	Mr John Emerson

The Said Gent. were Sworn Received there Charge and were Dismissed till ye next Court all but Mr James Moore

---

Whereof The Court of Generall Sessions of ye peace held at Worcester In and for the County of Worcester of ye Second Tuesday of august last past Did order that the House of m^r Daniel Haywood in Worcester Remain a Goal (for such persons as give bond for ye Liberty of ye Yard &c) till the further order of the Court &c The Court now order that said House Remain a Goal for the ends aforesaid no Longer Then the first day of June next, and that Such Prisoners as may be then Retained in Said house as prisoners that have the Liberty of the Yard be Removed by the Sheriff of ye County to his majestys Goal newly Erected and be there Retained under the Same Circumstances as now they are and the Sheriff is hereby ordered to Remove them accordingly

---

Elisha Johnson of Sutton In the County of Worcester Gent being presented by the Grandjurors for the body of the Said County at the Court of Generall Sessions of ye peace Held at Worcester In and for the County of Worcester on the Sixth day of Febry last past for not building and Keeping in Repair two bridges on the Two Branches of BlackStones River in ye bounds of Hassanamisco in ye County of Worcester as by his own Covenant and by law he ought which is against ye peace of our Lord ye King his Crown & Dignity and the good and wholesome laws of this Government &c^t and being bound over by m^r Justice Jenison To this Court to make answer To said Presentment now appeared and by his attorney m^r Edm^d Gouff al^r Trowbridge Comes into Court & Defend^s y^e [   ] & Injury &c^t and prays Judgment of ye presentment aforesaid for that the presentment aforesaid and the matter therein contained is Insufficient in law to maintain a presentment and to which the def^t by the law of the land is not bound to make answer and this he is ready to Verifie wherefore for the Insufficiency of ye presentment aforesaid ye Deft prays Judgment that he may be Dismissed, &c^t which pleas Together with ye answer of John Overing Esq attorney To our Sovereign Lord ye King being Duly Considered, The Court are of opinion that a presentment Lyes in this Case and the Said Elisha Johnson not maintaining his Demurer is adjudged by the Court Guilty according to the presentment and therefore order'd That he doe by the first day of august next Effectually Repair both Said Bridges or in default thereof That he pay as a fine to our Said Lord the King The Sum of Eighty pounds and Cost Taxed at   pounds   Shillings &   pence

The Said Elisha Johnson appealed from this Judgment to the next Court of assize & Generall Goal Delivery To be holden at Worcester in and for the County of Worcester In September next, & Entered into ye following Recognizance for prosecuting his appeal with Effect pursuant to law vizt The Said Elisha Johnson as principall In the Sum of one hundred pounds & Samuel Dudley Esq & Timothy Carter yeoman both of Sutton in the County of Worcester Suretys in the Sum of fifty pounds Each acknowledged themselves Severally Indebted in the aforesaid Sums to our Sovereign Lord the King to be Leveyed upon their Severall goods or Chattells Lands or Tenements for ye Use of said Lord the King or his Successors Conditioned that the said Elisha Johnson prosecute his appeal aforesaid with Effect.

Peter Corly of Leicester in ye County of Worcester husbandman being bound over To this Court by way of Recognizance To answer To his presentment by ye Grandjury for prophane Swearing &c̄t came into Court & pleaded Guilty Its therefore ordered by the Court that he pay as a fine To our Lord the King five Shillings & Costs, & Stand Committed till Sentance is performed which he paid in Court and was Dismissed

———

William McMichell & Margarett his wife of Woodstock In ye County of Worcester came into Court and Complained of themselves for being Guilty of ye Crime of fornication before marriage, were find Each Thirty Shillings To our Lord ye King & Costs which they paid & were Dismissed

———

Alexander Turner of Worcester & Mary his wife came into Court and complained of themselves for being Guilty of ye Crime of fornication before marriage, were find To our Lord ye King the Sum of Thirty Shillings, Each & Cost, which they paid & were dismissed

———

Solomon Johnson of Leicester in ye County of Worcester Gent being presented by the Grandjurors for being drunk[1] &c̄t, came into Court & put himself on Tryall and was acquited paying Cost which he paid & was Dismissed

———

Phillip Chase of Worcester In ye County of Worcester husbandman being presented by the Grandjurors for Working unecessaryly on the Lords day &c̄t came into Court & put himself upon Tryall by the Court & was acquitted paying Cost

---

[1] The penalty for drunkenness was a fine of five shillings; or in lieu thereof the offender was to sit in the stocks not exceeding three hours.

Dom Rex

vs

Rice

JURY

Mr James Keyes
Mr John Curtice
Mr John Biglo
Mr George Bruce
Mr Eben: How
Mr Jacob Amsden
Mr Jona Towne
Mr Joshua Convers
Mr Symon dakin
Mr John Bush
Mr Nathan Brigham
Mr Daniel Davis

Our Sovereign Lord yᵉ King pla' versus Perez Rice late of Westboro' In the County of Worcester now of Sutton in Said County Deft,

The Said Rice was now appel' from a Judgment given against him by mʳ Justice Ward for Lying or false Speaking

The Said appᵉˡᵗ appeared & pleaded not Guilty & the Case after a full hearing was Committed to the Jury who were Sworn according to law To Trye the Same and Return'd there Verdict in as follows vizᵗ That the appelt is not Guilty of Lying or false Speaking   The Court thereupon order That the Said Perez Rice be dismissed paying Costs which were accordingly paid   The Court Thereupon order That the fine of five Shillings be Remitted & yᵉ Sᵈ Justice ordered to pay the Same to the Sᵈ Rice

———

The Court proceeded to Examin & Sort the Votes Sent from the Severall Towns for yᵉ Choice of a County Treasurer & it appeared That Mʳ Benjamin Flagg Junʳ was Duly Elected & an oath was administered To him before the Court by the Clerk

———

The Court order that the County Treasurer Pay to yᵉ Comittee appointed for building yᵉ Goal Sixty five pounds being the last payment agreeable to there Contract & the further Sum of five pounds To pay for Such things as were omited in the Said Contract.

———

The Court now order that the Clerk Send forth a Scire facias agts Obadiah Colidge and his bondsmen to appear at the next Court of Genˡˡ Sessions of yᵉ peace to give reason why there bonds should not be declared forfiet also a warrant to bring him to his tryall for the Crime laid to his Charge

An acco^t of Nahum Ward Esqr for Service done ye County about the Goal amounting to thirty five Shillings Read and allowed & the Treas^r of ye County is according ordered To pay ye Same to the Said Nahum Ward Esq in full Discharge thereof

---

An acco^t of William Gray J^r late Constable for attendance on the Grandjury four days Read & Ordered that ye County Treasurer pay To ye Said William Gray J^r Sixteen Shillings in full discharge thereof

---

A Petition of Thomas Richardson of Leicester Shewing the Damage he Sustains by Reason of the Escape of Thomas Hall from his majestys Goal in Worcester where he was Comitted by Virtue of an Execution the petitioner had Served on him and that he apprehends it was thro' Some defect Either for want of a Sufficient Goal Goal Keeper &c praying for Releife Upon Reading this Petition m^r Sheriff Gookin came into Court and Informed them that he had lately heard that the within named Thomas Hall was in ye Colony of Connecticot and that he would Send out advertisements after him in order for his being Taken, Therefore ordered that the petition be Referred To ye next Court of Generall Sessions for further Consideration

---

A By law of the Town of Leicester being presented To this Court was Read and approved of by the Court for the Term of three year and is on file

---

At the Generall Sessions of the peace holden at Worcester within and for the County of Worcester on the Second Tuesday of may 1733 The Grandjury for the Body of the Said County Upon their Oaths do present John Jenings Husbandman and Elisabeth Jening Housewife wife of the Said John Jennings and Eliner Kellog Spinster all of Brookfield In ye County aforesaid Each and all of them for the Crime of fornication and Matthew Addleton Cooper and Thomas ainsworth Husbandman both of Brookfield aforesaid for Unnecessarily absenting themselves from ye publick worship of God on the Lords days for more than Two months last past and also Jonathan Waldo & Thomas Fayerweather Gent for Travelling Unnecessaryly on the last lords day from oxford to Worcester In the Said County and also the Town of Leicester for their not being provided with a writing & Reading School master all which things are against the peace of our Sovereign Lord the King his Crown & Dignity &c^t   Ebenezer Learned foreman

---

Mr Jonathan Waldo & Mr Thomas Fayerweather pleaded To ye Insufficiency of there presentment which being Duly Considered the Court ordered That they should be dismissed paying Cost which was paid.

The Petitions of ye Town of Sutton and Hassanamisco presented this Court at their Sessions in February last praying that the Road lately laid out by order of this Court leading from Worcester To Mendon &c^t   Read again together with ye answers of ye Towns of Mendon & Uxbridge and being Duly Considered ordered that Said Petitions So far as they Relate to the altering Said Road be Dismissed and the Said Road is by the Said Court fully absolutely Settled & Determined to be the County Road leading from Worcester to Mendon & ye Report or Return of ye Sheriff & Jury thereupon ordered to be Recorded

The acco^u of the Charge viewing & Laying out Said Road amounting unto the Sum of Thirty one pound Seven Shillings allowed of by the Court & is due To ye following persons vizt

To ye Comittee for viewing &c^t	7	1	10
To Mr Sheriff Gookin : 3£ 2/ To Justice Dudley			
attending on ye Jury 3S/	5	0	0
To the Jury Each 30/ 18£ : To ye Clerk writing : &c^t 25/2	19	5	2
	£31	7	0

The Court thereupon ordered that Said Charge be paid by the Respective Towns through [which] ye Said Road Runs Viz^t

The Town of Mendon To pay Seven pounds Eight Shillings & Sixpence	7	8	6
Uxbridge Thirty three Shillings	1	13	0
Hassanamisco Three pounds Six Shillings	3	6	0
Sutton Twelve pounds Seven Shillings & Sixpence	12	7	6
Worcester Six pounds Twelve Shillings	6	12	0
	£31	7	0

and order that the Clerk Serve ye Towns with a Copy of This order That they assess the Respective Sum Laid on them and that the Same be paid To William Jenison Esqr To be by him paid To ye persons to whom the Same is Respectively Due

The Return of ye Sheriff & Jury is as follows vizt

Worcester ss   To the Sheriff of the County of Worcester his under Sheriff or Deputy Greeting

Whereas the Committee lately appointed by his majestys Court of Gen^{ll} Sessions of y^e peace, for the County of Worcester have made Report Concerning a Publick Highway or County Road between the Towns of Worcester and Mendon being necessary and Convenient &c^t as $\wp$ their Report may appear

(L.S) These are therefore In his Majestys name to Require and Command you to Sumon a Jury of Good and lawfull men Quallyfyed according to law to meet & assemble at the House of Capt William Rawson in Mendon aforesaid on monday the Second day of October next which Jury So Sumoned or Impanneled you are to Cause a proper oath to be administered to them by a Justice of the peace for the County aforesaid and then proceed to view & lay out a Publick highway or County Road between the Towns aforesaid pursuant To the laws of this province and having a due Regard to the Report of the late Comittee

hereof fail not & make due Return hereof with your doings herein to this Court at their next Sessions of the peace to be held here on the first Tuesday of November next as well under your own hand as the hands of the Jury aforesaid Dated at Worcester this 25th day of September In the Sixth year of his majestys Reigne anno : Dom : 1732

By order of Court John Chandler J Cle pac Worcester October 2[d] 1732

1732 In Observance of the within written warrant I have Impannelled a Jury as the law directs who after being Sworn went upon the Spot and laid out the County Road from mendon meeting House to Worcester meeting House as ⅌ y[e] annexed Discription will appear under their hands

Daniell Gookin Sheriff—Worcester Octo 2[d] 1732

In Observance of an order of the Court of General Sessions of the peace for the County of Worcester held at Worcester by adjournment of the third Wednesday of September Last past ordered the Sheriff of S[d] County to Impoint a Jury of Good & Lawfull men & Have them Sworn before one of his majestys Justices of the peace of S[d] County to Lay out a Country Road from Mendon to Worcester meeting House Accordingly the Sheriff of S[d] County Hath Impointed a Jury as afores[d] whose names are Hereafter Subscribed & Legally Sworn have Layed out S[d] Country Road on oath as Hereafter Discribed Imprimis beginning at mendon meeting House as the Road now Lyeth until it comes to the House of Decon John Teilor & from thence to a Rhoad of four Rods wide until it Comes to the House of Robert Teilor from thence by the Westerly side of a meadow Called eight acre meadow from thence to a Small Black oak tree Standing on the edge of a brook near a great Rock near the House of John Sadler & from thence as the Road is now Drawn until it come to a Red oak tree marked upon [   ] near a Brook by Sam[ll] Woods Sawmil & from thence by marked trees to a very High Rock near the House of John Perim then Running between the House & barn of S[d] Perrim & So between the House & barn of Eleazer ffletcher, & So on till it Comes to the Land of Jacob Whipple & through S[d] Land till it comes to a White oak tree on the bank of the River So Crossing Blackstons River & running to a heap of Rocks in Isaac Chases Land & So on to a White oak tree near the House of John Ward

from thence Leading to the Country Road by the House of m^r
James Lealand then turning Westerly & Running by marked trees
till it comes to a Red oak tree Standing on the Land of Sam^{ll}
Chase & So on till it comes to a white oak tree Standing near the
Dwelling House of Frances Dudley So Running to a white oak tree
neare the House of Sam^{ll} Dudley Esq & So on to a Heap of Stones
& So by marks to Stump of a tree & a heap of Stones in Willm
Waits Land then Crossing the River by a black oak tree marked
& So Running on by the House of Skiper Fairfield by marked
trees till it Comes to the House of Deacon Natha^{ll} Moore in
Worcester & by the House of Jonas Rice thence to the House of
Tirus Rice & So running by the House of the Revr^d Mr Isaac Burr
untill it Comes to the meeting House in Worcester bounded being
on the Northerly & Easterly Side of S^d Road & S^d Road to be
four Rods on the Southwesterly Side afores^d Boundaries

Gershom Rice Jonas Rice James Keith William Rawson Joseph White Daniell Haywood James Holdin James Lealand
Joseph Crosby John Sibley John Sadler Robert Barber

Mr Jonathan Houghton County Treasurer presented his acco^{tt}
To the Court the ballance due to the County being twenty four
pounds 1/4   Read Ex^d & accepted & the Clerk ordered to
Signe the Same in the name of the Court,

Then ye Court was adjourned without day
att^s   John Chandler J Cler

WORCESTER ss *Anno R¹ Rˢ Georgij Secundi nunc Magnæ Brittainiæ et Hiberniæ Septimo* ⊃

Att his majestys Court of Generall Sessions of yᵉ peace begun and held at Worcester in and for the County of Worcester on the Second Tuesday of August being the 14ᵗʰ day of Said month Anno Dom : 1733

JUSTICES PRESENT

John Chandler	John Chandler Jun	Henry Lee
Joseph Wilder	Samˡ Wright	Nahum Ward
William Ward	Esqs Josiah Willard	Esqs
William Jenison	Joseph Dwight	
Danl Taft	Samˡ Dudley	

} Esqs

Grand jury that attended.

Mʳ Gershom Rice foreman
Capᵗ Richard Moore
Mʳ Hooker Osgood
Mʳ James Moore
Mʳ William Richardson
Mʳ Thomas Thayre
Mʳ Edward Morris
Capᵗ Wᵐ Old :
Mʳ David Maynard

Mʳ Samˡ Lillie
Mʳ Wᵐ Brown
Mʳ James Newton
Mʳ Moses How
Mʳ Richard Davenport
Mʳ John Emerson
Mʳ Samˡ Johnson
Mʳ Jonᵃ Farnsworth

Each attended 2 days Except Capᵗ Old who attended one day
Isaac Moore Constable 1 day

Worcester ss The Grandjurors of our Sovereign Lord the King
for the body of ye Said County at a Generall Sessions of ye peace
holden at Worcester within and for the said County of Worcester
on ye Second Tuesday of August 1733 upon their Oaths do present
That Jonathan Lamb Gent and Lydia Lamb Housewife and wife
of the Said Jonathan Lamb and Solomon Johnson Gent all of Leicester in Said County Each and all of them have absented themselves from the Publick Worship of God on ye Lords days for more
then Twelve weeks last past That Solomon Johnson aforesaid on
or about ye thirteenth day of July last past was Guilty of Drunkenness in Leicester aforesaid. That the Said Solomon Johnson on
ye 14th day of August Current did prophanely Swear in Worcester
in ye County aforesaid That Richard Wheeler of Worcester in
our Said County Housewright hath not attended the Publick Worship of God on ye Lords days for more than Eight weeks last past
That Daniel Eliott of Sutton in Said County husbandman on y^e
last Lords day being in Uxbridge did unnecessarily Travell To Sutton in Said County. That Rachell Wilder of Lancaster in Said
County Spinster on the first day of September last past was Guilty
of the Crime of Fornication in Lancaster aforesaid. That Joseph
Perry of Brookfield in Said County hath not attended ye Publick
Worship of God on Lords days for more than Eight weeks last
past all which severall actions of the Severall forenamed persons
are high Criminall and against ye peace of our Sovereign Lord
George by ye Grace of God of Great Britain France and Ireland
King Defender of the ffaith &c and the Good and wholsom laws
of this province   Joseph Dwight attorney pro Dom Reg^o
     Billa vera   Gershom Rice foreman

Richard Wheeler of Worcester in ye County of Worcester
Housewright being presented by the Grandjurors for ye body of y^e
County of Worcester To this present Court for not attending on
the Publick Worship of God on ye Lords days for more than Eight
weeks last past Came into Court and Confessed himself Guilty but
gave his Reasons therefor The Court thereupon order he be Dismissed paying Costs which he did & withdrew

James Nuting and Josiah Nuting both of Hassanamisco In ye County of Worcester husbandmen appeared in Court and to their presentment by ye Grandjurors for ye body of ye County of Worcester In Febry last past for Traveling Unecessarily on ye Saturday evening after Sun Sett before the Lords day from Lancaster to Groton pleaded not Guilty & putt him Self on Tryall by the bench and after a full hearing The Court ordered they Should be discharged paying Cost wch they p^d

---

Mathew Addleton of Brookfield in ye County of Worcester, Cooper being presented by ye Grandjurors for ye body of ye County of Worcester in may last for Unnecessaryly absenting himself from ye Publick worship of God &ct appeared in Court & pleaded Guilty Whereupon ye Court ordered him To pay a fine to our Sovereign Lord ye King of five Shillings & Cost of prosecution Standing Comitted till Sentance be performed which he paid & was discharged

---

John Elisons Recognizance was Discharged.

Paul Rich's Recognizance Discharged

Eleaner Kellog being bound over by way of Recognizance by m^r Justice Dwight To answer To her presentment by the Grandjurors &ct for her being Guilty of ye Crime of fornication appeared in Court and pleaded Guilty of having a bastard Child born of her body The Court Thereupon ordered that She pay as a fine to our Sovereign Lord ye King The Sum of five pounds or be whipt on the naked body Ten stripes & pay Cost of prosecution, ye fine & Cost were paid and her Recognizance Discharged

---

Martha McKintree of Dudley Spinster being bound by way of Recognizance to appear at ye Court of Gen^ll Sessions of ye peace

held here in may last To answer for being Guilty of Fornication
and not being able To Travell then her bonds were Continued To
this Court She now appeared in Court pleaded Guilty whereupon the Court Order That for her Crime She pay a fine of four
pounds to our Sovereign Lord the King pay Costs of prosecution
and Stand Comitted till Sentance be performed The fine & Costs
were paid

The Town of Leicester being presented to the Court in may
last for not being provided with a writing & Reading Schoolmaster
as ye law Requires appeared by their Selectmen & it appearing
that they are now provided they were Exempted They paying
Costs

Timothy Sewell of Mendon in ye County of Worcester &c^t husbandman being bound over to this Court by m^r Justice Taft with
Two Suretys To answer to Such things as Should be Objected
against him on his majestys behalf Relateing To a Complaint
against him by Eben^r Cook of Mendon &c^t and failing of appearing the Recognizance was by the Court declared forfeited
and the Clerk ordered To Send out a Scire facias against ye Said
Sewall & his Suretys to appear at the next Court of Gen^ll Sessions
of ye peace to be holden here in Novr next To give Reason if any
they have wherefore Execution Should not be awarded against
them &c^t

Samuel Wadkins of Hopkinton in ye County of midlesex &c^t
Joyner al^s Husbandman being bound over to this Court by m^r Justice Tafft with Two Suretys to answer To Such Things as should
be objected [against] him on his majestys behalf Relateing to a
Complaint made against [him] by one Samuel Woods of mendon
&c^t, and failing of appearing the Recognizance was by ye Court
declared forfeited and ye Clerk ordered To Send out a Scire facias

against Said Wadkins & his bondsmen To apear at ye Court of Gen^ll Sessions of ye peace in Novr next To give Reason if any they have wherefore Execution Should not be awarded against them

---

The Select men of the Town of Worcester Returned a warrant whereby they had warned one Thomas Peirce with his wife martha & four Children namely Heaty John Nicholas & Thomas to depart the Town it being probable they be become a Town Charged which was approved off & is on file

---

Thomas Green & Danl Deny Return'd a list of ye Baptists in Leicester according To ye Order of Court of Febry 1731/2 approved off as also the list from Sutton

---

A Petition of ye Rev^d m^r David Parsons of Leicester Seting forth ye necesaty of Road or way being laid out leading from Rutland to Leicester from meeting House to meeting house praying Effectual Care may be taken to settle a way there as ye law Directs. Read, as also a petition of Daniel Deny & John Whitemore against Said petition being acted upon, also Read ; and In answer thereto ye Court order that Said Petitions be Refered to the next Court of Gen^ll Sessions of ye peace to be holden here in november next and In the mean time the Court appoint William Ward & Saml Wright Esqr^s and Capt Ebenezer Learned of oxford to be a Comittee to view ye lands in and between the Towns of Rutland and Leicester and make Report To the Said Court what may be proper to be Done in the premises.

An acco^tt of William Calwell Late Constable of Worcester for Attending on the grandjury amounting to Thirty two Shillings. Read and allowed of by the Court and the County Treasurer is accordingly ordered to pay the Same

The Honourable John Chandler Esqr made a motion to ye Court Informing them of ye necessaty of a County Road being laid out from ye Road leading from Worcester To Mendon lately Established by this Court & the Southern bounds of the Town of Dudley to the bounds of Conneƈticott Colony & also of ye Diffi-culty persons Travelling To the Shire Town from the Southward parts of ye County Lye under for want of a Sutable & Convenient Road moveing for Remedy, The Court having Considered ye matter Order & appoint That William Jenison Esqr Capt Richard Moore & Cap^{tt} Ebenezer Edmunds be a Comittee To view & make Report what they think proper for the Court To aƈt hereon, and they are desired to Report To the Court of Generall Sessions of ye peace In november next

---

Ordered that the Clerk of ye Court Signe an order Direƈting ye County Treasurer from time to time to pay To ye Comittees for building The Court house & Prisons Respeƈtively Such Sums of money as are Still due according to their Contraƈts for building the Same and also what may be due for Such ffurther aditions as are made over and above ye originall Contraƈts

WORCESTER ss *Anno Regni Regis Georgij Secundi nunc Magnæ Brittainiæ Franciæ et Hiberniæ Septimo* ⌒

Att a Court of Generall Sessions of ye peace begun and held at Worcester within and for the County of Worcester on the first Tuesday of November being the Sixth day of Said month Annoq Dom: 1733

PRESENT

John Chandller Esq	Joseph Wilder Esq	William Ward Esq
William Jenison Esq	Danl Taft Esq	Samuel Dudley Esq
Joseph Dwight Esq	Nahum Ward Esq	John Chandller Jr Esq

———

Names of ye Grandjurors that attended.

Mr Gershom Rice foreman
Capt Richard Moore
Mr Hooker Osgood
Mr James Moore
Mr William Richardson
Mr Thomas Thayre
Mr Edward Moris
Capt Wm Old :

Mr David Maynard
Mr Saml Lillie
Mr Wm Brown
Mr James Newton
Mr Moses How
Mr Richard Davenport
Mr Saml Johnson
Mr Jon^a Farnsworth

Each attended Two days and Constable Isaac Moore 2 days

Worcester ss att a Generall Sessions of ye Peace holden at Worcester within and for the County of Worcester on Tuesday ye Sixth day of November anno Domini 1733, The Grandjurors for ye body of ye Said County upon their Oaths do presentt ; That Dudley Jordan and Benjamin Smith both of Lambs Town[1] as So Called in Said County Husbandman did on ye 28th day of october last past being ye Lords day Unnecessaryly Travell through ye Town of Shrewsbury In Said County—and also that   the wife of Thomas Hutchins of Dudley in Said County hath Unnecessaryly absented herself from the from ye Publick Worship of God on ye Lords days for more than Two months last past. and also That David Haynes of Sudbury in ye County of Midlesex Gent and Samuel Waldo of Boston in ye County of Suffolk merchant and George Mareiss of Boston aforesaid Waiter did each and all of them Unecessaryly Travell from Rutland to Worcester On ye Lords day being ye 23^d day of September last past—and also that Samuel Bridges Husbandman & Mary Godman Housewife and Mehittable Bridges Spinster all of Mendon in ye County of Worcester and Bethhya Gassett of Southborough in Said County Spinster Each and all of them for Unecessaryly absenting themselves from ye Publick Worship of God for more then Two months last past ; and also that Daniel Taft of Mendon in ye County of Worcester Esqr about Six weeks Since at ye House of William Jenison Esqr in Worcester in Said County did Wittingly and Willingly make and Spread a false Report against Samuel Terry of Mendon aforesaid Clerk with Intent to abuse and deceive ye Said Terrey and Others by Saying that m^{rs} Rawson Told him y^t the Said Terrey was so bad of it (meaning that he was So disguised with drink that he was led or put To bed on one Scacrament day night and that Grindall Rawson and m^r Dorr were ye persons that put him To bed all which things are against the peace of our Sovereign Lord George by ye Grace of God of Great Britain France and Ireland King defender of ye faith &c and ye Good and wholsome laws of this province   Joseph Dwight attorney pro Rego
  Gershom Rice foreman
                    Entered P̃ Jno Chandler J^r Cle pac

---

[1] Now Hardwick.

Amariah Bush's Recognizance Discharged
Nathaniel Waits Recognizance Discharged
Abigaill Lesure Recognizance Discharged &ct
Sam^ll Terrey Clerk Complaint against Abigal Lesure withdrawn
Samuel Wadkins Recognizance discharged
Timothy Sewell Recognizance Discharged

William Ward Esqr one of ye Comittee To whom the Petition of the Revered m^r David Parsons was present to ye Court in august last past was comitted made a report, whereon Upon ye Court order that the affair Relating thereto Lye till ye further order of this Court

---

A vote or By Law of ye Town of Woodstock being presented to ye Court for their allowance and approbation ye Same was accordingly approved off and is on file

---

A memoriall of Thomas Palmer Esqr Seting forth y^t ye Jury in laying out the way To Mendon runs it through his Orchyard & mowing land & not agreeable To ye Report of ye Comittee which is as he apprehends through a mistake pray the Said mistake may be Rectified &ct Read and ordered that the Said memoriall & ye Subject matter thereof be Comitted To William Jenison & Henry Lee Esq^rs That they view ye Road where ye mistake is Supposed To be done & Report as Soon as may be what they may think proper for the Court to doe thereupon.

An acco^tt of Daniel Gookin Esqr Sheriff of ye County of Worcester amounting unto ye Sum of Twenty Two pounds three Shillings for Sundry Services & Sallary &ct as ℈ ye acco^tt appears Read & Examined and order that the Said acco^t be allowed & The Treasurer of ye County is accordingly ordered To [pay] ye Said Sum of Twenty Two pounds three Shillings To Daniel Gookin Esqr in full Discharge thereof.

Samuel Terrey of Mendon in the County of Worcester Clerk appellant from a Sentance given against him by Daniel Taft Esqr one of his majestys Justices of the peace for Said County Upon yᵉ Complaint or information of William Torrey of Mendon aforesaid Husbandman on his majestys behalf for his the Said Terrys being Drunk in yᵉ Town of Mendon &ᶜt whereby he was Sentanced To pay a fine for the Use of yᵉ poor of yᵉ Town of Mendon yᵉ Sum of five Shillings & fees & Cost of Sute &ᶜt as ℘ yᵉ Complaint The Sentance appears and now yᵉ appellant appeared and put him Self upon Tryall of his plea of not Guilty by the Court The Evidences in behalf of our Sovereign Lord yᵉ King were Sworn & yᵉ Case fully and maturely heard Its Therefore Considered by the Court That the former Sentance be Confirmed & that therefore yᵉ Said Samuel Terrey pay as a fine To yᵉ Use of yᵉ poor of yᵉ Town of Mendon The Sum of five Shillings with former and additional Costs and Stand comitted untill This Sentance be performed, yᵉ fine & Costs were paid in Court & yᵉ appelᵗ Dismissed

---

Ebenʳ Albee of Mendon &ᶜt appelᵗ from a Judgment given against him by William Jenison Esqr as appears by yʳ Judgmᵗ on file, This Case was comitted to the Jury and it appearing To be a mistryal inasmuch as yᵉ Jury Seperated before they had agreed upon a Verdict Therefore yᵉ Court order That This Case be Continued To yᵉ 1ˢᵗ Tuesday of Febry next of which all persons Concerned are To take notice and Conform them Selves accordingly

---

Tom Negro of Leicester In the County of Worcester Labourer Servant of Capᵗ Thomas Steel of Boston Gent being presented by yᵉ Grandjurors for the body of the County aforesaid for yᵗ yᵉ Said Tom Negro being at Worcester aforesaid on or about yᵉ 22ᵈ day of September last past did find a Certain Pockett book or Case with a Three pound Bill and one Ten Shilling Bill and a letter therein all which things belonged to Ralph Earl of Leicester in Said County Yeoman and yᵉ Said things yᵉ Said Tom having So

found did and doth Still negleél & Refuse to enter with yᵉ Town
Clerk Cry and post as yᵉ law Requires all which is against yᵉ peace
of our Lord yᵉ King his Crown & Dignity & yᵉ good and Wholsome laws of this province as appears by yᵉ presentment   The
said Tom Negro came into Court & pleaded To yᵉ Insufficiency
of yᵉ presentment as p̃ yᵉ pleas on file which were over-Ruled and
the said Tom Negro pleaded not Guilty & put himself upon Tryall
by yᵉ Court,   The witnesses In the Case were Sworn and the matter being duly Considered the Court are of opinion that the Said
Tom Negro found the Three pound bill and The Ten Shilling bill
as sett forth in yᵉ presentment and yᵉ pockett book of yᵉ Value of
one Shilling and that he hath negleéled Entering crying and post-
ing up the Same according to law   That therefore the Said Tom
Negro Hath forfeited to yᵉ use of yᵉ poor of yᵉ Town of Leicester
The sum of Twenty three Shillings & Eight pence for his negleél :
& yᵗ pay yᵉ Sum of three pounds Eleven Shillings To yᵉ Said Ralph
Earl being yᵉ money found & yᵉ Value of yᵉ Book and pay Costs
Standing Comitted Till This Sentance be performed. The Said Tom
Negro appealed from This Sentance To yᵉ next Court of assize and
General Goal delivery To be holden at Worcester in and for yᵉ County
of Worcester on the wednesday Imediately preceeding The time
by law appointed for holding Said Court of assize and Generall
Goal delivry at Springfield in and for the County of Hampshire
in September next and entered into Recognizance with Two Suffi-
cient Suretys to prosecute his appeal with Effeél. –Tom Negro of
Leicester In yᵉ County of Worcester Labourer as principall In yᵉ
Sum of Twenty pounds and Thomas Steel Junʳ of Boston In yᵉ
County of Suffolk Gent and Edmund Goff alˢ Trowbridge of Cambridge in the County of Midlesex Gent as Suretys In Ten pounds
Each acknowledged themselves bound by way of Recognizance To
our Sovereign Lord yᵉ King his heirs and Successors to be Leveyed
on their Severall goods or Chattells lands or Tenements for the use
of our Lord yᵉ King Conditioned that the Said Negro Tom prosecute his appeal as aforesaid with Effeél

                  attʳ   John Chandler Jʳ Cle pac

Our Sovereign Lord the King pla' versus Obadiah Coolidge of marlbro' In the County of midlesex Cordwainer Versus William Taylor & abraham Eager Jun' both of Shrewsbury In the County of Worcester Deft' as ꝑ a Scire facias Served on them & duly Returned dated July 2ᵈ 1733, appears. and now yᵉ Said Obadiah Coolidge who was the principal did not appear but the said William Taylor & abraham Eager yᵉ Suretys appeared and pleaded in abatement of yᵉ process as appears by yᵉ pleas which being duly Considered by the Court Its ordered that yᵉ writt of Scire facias abate

12

WORCESTER ss   *Anno R¹ Rˢ Georgij Secundi nunc Magnæ Britaniæ Franciæ et Hiberniæ Septimo*

Att a Court of Generall Sessions of yᵉ peace begun and held at Worcester within and for the County of Worcester on the first Tuesday of February being the fifth day of Said month Annoq Dom. 1733/ :—

JUSTICES PRESENT

John Chandler Esqʳ	Danl Taft Esqʳ	Joseph Dwight Esqʳ
Joseph Wilder Esqʳ	John Chandler Jr Esqʳ	Samˡ Dudley Esqʳ
William Ward Esqʳ	Samuel Wright Esqʳ	Nahum Ward Esqʳ
William Jenison Esqʳ	Henry Lee Esqʳ	Edward Hartwell Esqʳ
		John Keyes Esqʳ

Grandjury that attended were

Mʳ Gershom Rice foreman	Mʳ Thoˢ Thayer
Capᵗ Richard Moore	Mʳ Edward Morris
Mʳ Hooker Osgood	Capᵗ William Old
Mʳ James Moore	Mʳ David Maynard
Mʳ Samuel Lillie	Mʳ Richard Davenport
Mʳ William Brown	Mʳ Samˡ Johnson
Mʳ James Newton	Mʳ Jonathan Farnsworth
Mʳ Moses How	Mʳ John Emerson

Each attended 2 days and Isaac Moore Constable also

The presents are on file

The Court order that for ye future and untill ye further order this Court that Thursday be ye day more Imediately Set a part for ye Doing of Sessions business

———

John Jennings of Brookfield In ye County of Worcester Husbandman and Elizabeth Jenings his wife being presented by the Grandjurors &c^t for ye Crime of fornication appeared & Confessed themselves Guilty were find Each fourty Shillings To ye King wch they pay'd & also Cost and were Dismissed

———

Peter Marville of Mendon In ye County of Worcester Physitian being presented by ye Grandjurors &c^t as ꝑ ye presentment appears, appeared and pleaded to the Insufficiency of ye presentment, which being duly considered ordered That ye presentment be Quashed & ye Said Marville was Dismissed paying Cost

———

Samuell Crawford of Hassamisco In ye County of Worcester weaver appellant from a Judgment given ag^st him by John Chandler J^r Esqr, as ꝑ ye Judgt & recognizance appears came into Court & fulfilled ye Judgm^t of ye Justice & leave himself on ye mercy of the Court, he was Dismissed paying Costs &c^t

———

Daniel Eliott J^r of Sutton &c^t being presented by ye Grandjurors for Rideing on the Lords day as ꝑ ye presentment appears appeared and was Dismissed paying Cost

———

Benjamin Davis also Ephraim Haywood & Jonas Haywood the Recognizances Discharged by order of Court

———

A Report of William Jenison Esqr & Eben^r Edmunds Two of a Comittee appointed by this Court in august last past to view &

Report to this Court concerning ye laying out a Country Road leading from the Country Road lately Established by S^d Court from Worcester to mendon to the Southerly bounds of ye Town of Dudley &ct made Report of their doings which were Read & accepted and ordered To lye on file & the Charge thereof being five days to William Jenison Esqr fifty Shillings & four days to Eben^r Edmunds fourty Shillings & their Expenses being fourty Shillings also allowed

----

The Selectmen of Brookfield presented to ye Court ye warning of margarett m^cTroy with her Child Danl m^cTroy also James Tute and his wife Kesiah Tute with their Children vizt mary Tute thankfull Tute and amos Tute, as p^r ye warrant warning &ct appears and is on file

----

The Select men of ye Town of Southboro' under their hands Informed this Court that one John Steer & his wife late from the Kingdom of Ireland, &ct had been warned out of their Return, praying Caution may be Entered thereof as p^r ye Information on file appears

----

The Selectmen of the Town of Harvard presented a warrant which was Executed by John Daly Constable of S^d Town, whereby Seth Colwes & his wife & Children were warned To Depart Said Town. which is on file

----

A Vote or By law of ye Town of Rutland was presented to this Court by Sam^ll Wright Esqr In behalf of Said Town vizt, Att a Town meeting of the Inhabitants of Rutland legally warned December 12th 1733. & Vote in Said meeting that a Tax of five Shillings p^r head shall be laid on all horses & neat Cattle that be brought into the Town of Rutland to Graze or Sumer there by any person or persons other then proprietors and they for any other then proprietors Cattle or horses or oxen hired to work or Cows to give

milk and that if any person or persons living in or belonging to
Rutland aforesaid Shall bring in or take any Strangers Cattle or
horses brought into Said Town to keep or take Care or Charge of
Such Creatures Shall be obliged to Render an acco^{tt} upon oath
what & how many Such horses or Cattle they have y^e Charge of
or Knowing to and Shall pay five Shillings $\tilde{p}$ head for all Such
horses or Cattle as are in their Care or Charge the money to be
for the use of y^e Town and this act to be laid before the Justices
at y^e next Quarter Sessions to be held at Worcester for y^e County
of Worcester for their Confirmation, Voted that Samuell Wright
Esqr is Chosen by the Town to lay ye above Written act before y^e
Said Court for Confirmation Samuel Wright moder^r,

which is accepted alowed & approved of ye Justices &^{ct}

Lydia Lamb Recog' Discharged
Jonathan Lamb Recognizance Discharged
John Hambleton Recognizance Discharged
Samuell Bridges Recog' Discharged

Solomon Johnson of Leicester being presented by ye Grandjurers for ye Crime of Drunkeness, was bound to appear at ye Court,
did appear, and there being no Evidences against him was Dismissed paying Cost which was 38/6

Solomon Johnson above being presented by ye Grandjurors for
unecessaryly absenting him Self from ye publick Worship of God
& bound To answer it at this Court appeared and ye Evidences
not being to be had he was dismissed paying Cost wch was 38/6

Solomon Johnson above being presented by the Grandjurers for
ye Crime of prophane Swearing ye Evidences not appearing he was
dismissed paying Cost wch was 38/6

Solomon Johnson above appelant from Judgment of William
Ward Esqr appeared & Submitted ye matter To ye Court who Confirmed former Judgment with additional Cost ye whole being 54/
& ye fine 5,

The Court order that there be a County Tax or assessment amounting unto the Sum of one hundred & fifty Seven pounds Eight Shillings & nine pence Raised on the Severall Towns within this County for defraying the usuall necessary Charges arising with the Same and that the Clark of this Court forthwith Send out warrants To yᵉ Select men or assessors of yᵉ Respective Towns for assessing their Severall parts or proportions thereof according to yᵉ rule for assessing the province Charges as the law direct & for paying in the Same to Capt Benjamin Flagg County Treasurer at or before the last day of may next ensueing.

The Severall Towns proportion thereof is as follows —vizt

Worcester	Eleven pound Seven Shillings & Eight pence	11	7	8
Lancaster	Twenty Six pound three Shillings & four pence	26	3	4
Mendon	Eighteen pound	18		
Woodstock	Sixteen pound	16		
Brookfield .	thirteen pound Ten Shilling & Eight pence	13	10	8
Southboro	Eight pound thirteen Shilling	8	13	0
Westboro'	Nine pound one Shilling	9	1	0
Leicester	Six pound nineteen Shillings & Eight pence	6	19	8
Shrewsbury	Seven pound Seven Shillings	7	7	
Sutton	Twelve pound five Shillings	12	5	
Oxford	Seven pound Two Shilling	7	2	
Uxbridge	Six pound & fourpence	6	0	4
. Rutland	three Pound Eighteen Shillings	3	18	0
Lunenburg	three pound Eighteen Shillings	3	18	
Harvard	Seven pound Three Shillings & one peny	7	3	1
	Sum Total	157	8	9

And warrants were accordingly Issued out march 1ˢᵗ 1733/4

attˢ   John Chandler Cle : pac

Jonathan Lamb of Leicester In yᵉ County of Worcester Gentˡ. being Complained of by mʳ Richard Davenport and mʳ William Brown two of the present Grandjurymen for this County &ct In behalf of them Selves & Said Grandjurors as well in behalf of our Lord the King that yᵉ Said Jonath Lamb about Ten days Since in yᵉ Town of Shrewsbury in Said County and at other times did abuse

and Defame ye Said Grandjurors by Saying that they were perjured
&ct against ye peace, being by order of Court by warrant from y^e
Clark brought To answer to Said Complaint, acknowledged the
facts laid against him whereupon the Court adjudged the Said
Jonathan Lamb was Guilty of abuseing ye Grandjurors aforesaid,
and the Said Jonathan Lamb behaving himself in a Rude & dis-
orderly maner in ye Court, the Court [order] that he be Comitted
To his majestys Goal there to Remain Till ye further order of this
Court and he was accordingly Comitted, and upon his humble and
hearty Concern for his offences as Expressed in his petition praying ye favour of ye Court &ct, the Court order that for his Said offences he pay a fine to the King of fourty Shillings & pay Cost &
fees & to Stand Comitted till this Sentance is performed   which
he paid in Court

Samuell Terry of Mendon in ye County of Worcester Clerk appellant from a Sentance given against him by Daniel Taft Esqr
one of his majestys Justices of the peace for the Said County Upon a Complaint or Information of William Torrey of Mendon afore-

TERRY
VS
DOM REX
JURY

Mr James Holding
Mr Ph: Haywood
Mr David Osgood
Mr Eb: Walker
Mr Joseph Lyon
Mr Hopestill Hinds
Capt Eb: Edmunds
Mr Jno Muttin
Mr Na: Parks
Mr D. Hubard
Mr Aaron Rice
Mr Wm Holoway

said Husbandman on his majestys behalf for
his ye Said Terrys being drunk in the Town of
Mendon &ct whereby he was Sentenced to pay
a fine for ye use of ye poor of the Town of
Mendon five Shillings & Cost & fees as ⅌ y^e
Complaint & Sentance of Said Justice appears
This appeal was originally brought To ye Court
of Generall Sessions of ye peace held here on
the first Tuesday of Novr last when & where
ye Sentence of Said Justice was Confirmed &ct
and upon ye Said Samuel Terry Adressing him-
self To ye Great & Genl Court or assembly of ye province he was
Enabled now again to prosecute his appeal as ⅌ ye order of Said
Court of Jan^ry last past appears, and now the Said Samuell Terry
appeared and pleaded not Guilty and the Case being fully argued
& heard it was Comitted To ye Jury who were Sworn according to

law To trye the Same & Returned their Verdict in that ye Said
Samuell Terry is not Guilty The Court Therefore order Rever-
sion of ye former Judgment & that the Said Samuell Terry be discharged paying Cost & fees Taxed at Seven pound and upon his
neglecting so to do the Court order Execution to be awarded for
ye Same and that it be paid into ye hands of the Clark of this Court
to be by him paid to whom the Same is due

DOM REX
vs
EB. ALBEE

Same Jury as in ye case
above

Ebenezer Albee of mendon in ye County of
Worcester Husbandman appel^t from a Judgment or Sentance given against him by William
Jenison Esq one of his majestys Justices of y^e
peace for Said County Upon ye Complaint of Samuell Terrey of
mendon in Said County Clark on his majestys behalf as well as of
his own as ᵽ ye Complaint appears & Sentance was given by Said
Justice y^t ye Said Eb albee pay a fine of Ten Shillings to ye use of
ye poor of mendon & Cost as ᵽ Sentence will appear and now y^e
Said Ebenezer Albee appearing and pleaded not Guilty, The Jury
being Sworn according to law, The Case after a full hearing on
both Sides was Comitted To the Jury To Trye ye Same who Returned there Verdict therein as follows vizt Not Guilty Its therefore Considered by the Court that the Sentence of ye Said William
Jenison Esqr be Reversed and that the Said Ebenezer Albee be
Discharged pay ffees & Costs which ffes and Costs is Taxed at
fourteen pounds Eighteen Shillings *and upon his neglecting to pay*
the Same The Court order Execution to be awarded for the Same
and that it be paid into ye hands of ye Clerk of this Court to be
by him paid to whom the Same is due

Sep^t. 16 : Satisfied   att^s John Chandler J Cl

TORREY
vs
DOM. REX

Same Jury as in ye
Other Cases

William Torrey of Mendon in the County of
Worcester app^lt from a Sentence given against
him by William Jenison Esqr one of his majestys Jus' of ye peace for Said County upon y^e
Complaint or Information of Samuel Terrey of Mendon in Said

County Clerk who did Complain on his majestys behalf as well as
of his own That about ye month of October last past before y^e
Complaint at mendon aforesaid ye Said William Torrey being
minded to abuse Scandalize & defame ye Complain^t did then &
there wittingly & willingly Publish a Lye of ye Complain^t &c^t by
Saying he had drunk & he could prove it or Sware to it or words
to that Effect or Import as p̃^l ye Complaint at large appears & the
appel^t was Sentenced to pay a fine to ye King Ten Shillings and
pay ffees & Cost &c^t. and now ye appel^t appeared and to Said
Complaint pleaded not Guilty. The Evidences on ye part of the
King being Sworn & the Case fully heard It was Comitted To y^e
Jury who were Sworn according to law To Trye the Same & Re-
turn'd their verdict therin upon oath vizt That ye said William
Torrey is not Guilty Its therefore Considered by the Court that
the Sentence of the Said Justice be reversed & that ye Appel^t be
Discharged paying Cost, Taxed at Twenty pound nine Shillings &
Sixpence but upon his neglecting to pay ye Same The Court order
Execution to be awarded for the Same and that it be paid into y^e
hands of ye Clark of this Court to be by him paid To whom y^e
Same is due

GOWEN
vs
DOM. REX

Same Jury as in y^e
Other Cases

Benjamin Gowen of Sutton in ye County of
Worcester Yeoman app^h from Sentence given
against him by John Chandler Junr Esqr one
of his majestys [justices] of ye peace for Said
County upon the Complaint of Robert Jenison of Said Sutton Yeoman who Complained on his majestys behalf as well as of his own
&c^t and by Said Sentence ye now appel^t was sentenced to pay as
a fine to our Sovereign Lord ye King five Shillings & pay Costs &
fees &c^t as p̃^l ye warrant and Sentence of Said Justice fully appears
—and now ye appel^t appeared & to the S^d Complaint pleaded not
Guilty the Case being fully & largely argued & heard It was Comitted to ye Jury who were Sworn according to law To Trye ye Same
& Return'd there Virdict therein upon Oath that is To Say The
said Benjamin Gowen is not Guilty Its therefore Considered by the

Court that the Sentence of yᵉ Justice shall be reversed and that yᵉ appelt be Discharged paying Cost Taxed at Nine pound Two Shillings & four pence and upon his negleƈting to pay yᵉ Same the Court order Execution to be awarded for yᵉ Same and that it be paid into the hands of yᵉ Clark of this Court to be by him paid To whome yᵉ Same is due   Exᵉ July 11 : 1734

NEWELL
vs
DOM REX

JURY

Mr James Holding
Mr Phi- Haywood
Mr David Osgood
Mr Benja Craggin
Mr Hopestill Hinds
Mr Samuel Beamons
Mr John Matthis
Mr Na. Parks
Mr Danl Hubbard
Mr Aaron Rice
Mr Wm Holoway
Mr Ob: Walker

Thomas Newell of Dudley in yᵉ County of Worcester Cordwainer appˡᵗ from a Sentence given against him by John Chandler J Esqʳ one of his majestys Justices of yᵉ peace for Said County upon yᵉ Complaint of John Runel of Said Dudley Joyner who Complained on his majestys behalf as well as of his own &ƈt for that yᵉ Sᵈ Newell being minded to abuse & defame yᵉ Complaᵗ &ƈt Did Wittingly & willingly make and Publish a Lye of yᵉ Complainᵗ &ƈt & Sentence was that he pay as a fine to his majesty Ten Shillings &ƈt & pay Cost & ffees &ƈt as ℔ yᵉ Sentence of Sᵈ Justice fully appears dated Decʳ. 12 : 1733. & now yᵉ appˡᵗ appeared and pleaded not Guilty & yᵉ Case being fully heard It was Comitted to yᵉ Jury who were Sworn according to Law to Trye yᵉ Same & Return'd there Verdiƈt therein upon oath vizt that yᵉ Said Thomas Newell is not Guilty Its therefore Considered by the Court the Sentence of the Sᵈ Justice be reversed and that yᵉ appˡᵗ be discharged paying Cost Taxed at Twenty one pound three Shillings & Six pence and upon his negleƈting to pay yᵉ Same yᵉ Court order Execution to be awarded and that it be paid into yᵉ hands of yᵉ Clark of this Court to be by him paid to whom it is due

WORCESTER ss   *Anno R^i R^s Georgij Secundi nunc Magnæ Britaniæ Franciæ et Hiberniæ Septimo*

Att a Court of Generall Sessions of the peace begun and held at Worcester within and for the County of Worcester on The Second Tuesday of May being the fourteenth day of Said month Annoq Dom 1734—

JUSTICES PRESENT

John Chandler Esqr ⎫ Justices of
Joseph Wilder Esqr ⎱ the Peace
William Ward Esqr   ⎰ &
William Jenison Esqr ⎭ Quorum
Daniel Taft Esqr
John Chandler Jr Esqr

Joseph Dwight Esqr
Samuel Dudley Esqr
Henry Lee Esqr
Nahum Ward Esqr
Samuel Willard Esqr
John Keyes Esqr

Grandjurors that attended this Court

Mr Gershom Rice foreman
Capt Richard Moore
Mr Hooker Osgood
Mr James Moore
Mr William Richardson
Mr Thomas Thayer
Mr William Old
Mr David Maynard

Mr Samuel Lillie
Mr William Brown
Mr James Newton
Mr Moses How
Mr Richard Davenport
Mr John Emerson
Mr Samuel Johnson
Mr Jonathan Farnsworth

Each attended Two days & Dep^t Sheriff with them

Names of the new Grandjurors who were Sworn and the Charge given them & then Dismissed till the Court of Generall Sessions of the peace in aug^st next vizt

Mr Joshua Child foreman ⎫   Mr Thomas Gleason Oxford
Mr Jotham Rice   ⎭ Worcester
Mr Josiah White   ⎫   Mr Benjamin Johnson Leicester
Mr Bazeliell Sawyer ⎭ Lancaster Mr Daniel Warren Westboro'
Mr Jonathan Bugbee Woodstock Mr Isaac Amsden Southboro'
Mr Joseph Sumner Mendon   Mr William Taylor Shrewsbury
Capt Thomas Gilbert Brookfield Mr Eleazer Ball Rutland
Mr Eben^r Read Uxbridge   Mr Nathan Heywood Lunenburg
Mr Joseph Sibly Sutton   Mr Simon Stone Harvard

David Haynes of Sudbury In the County of Midlesex Gent being presented by the Grandjurors for Unecessaryly Rideing on the Lords day ye 23^d day of Septem^r last & bound to this Court to answer his presentment pleaded to the Insufficiency of the presentment which was alowed of by ye Court & he dismissed paying Costs

---

An acco^tt of the Grandjurors Travell and attendance from may : 1733 To this time amounting to ye Sum of Seventy Eight pounds Eighteen Shillings presented for allowance which was according allowed of and ordered that the Clerk Certifie ye Same To ye County Treas^r for payment

---

The Court order that ye Treasurr be directed To pay The Sum of fourty Shillings To Isaac Moore a Constable for his attendance on The Grandjurors the year past vizt Ten days

---

Cap^tt Benj^a Flagg County Treas^r presented his acco^tts which were Examined & allowed of by the Court the ballance Due to ye County being thirteen pounds nineteen Shillings & Eight pence & ordered the Clerk To Sign ye Same

The Court order that ye Expenses of ye Comittee ab^t ye Court House being thirteen Shillings be paid out of ye County Treasury & that ye Clerk Certifie ye Same.

Ezekiel Upham Resident in Hassanamisco in ye County of Worcester Housewright appelant from a Sentance given against him by Nahum Ward Esqr one of his majestys Justices of ye peace for Said County Upon ye Complaint of Peter Lawrance Indian Planter of Hassanamisco aforesaid who Complained on his majestys behalf as well of his own &c̄t for his Taking five or Six bushells of Indian Corn out of a Corn Cribb in Hassanamisco aforesaid of his the Said Lawrances in a thiefish maner Sometime in the Winter past &c̄t & Sentence was that ye Said Upham is Guilty of Taking two bushells of the Corn he was Charged with in a theifish maner which Corn was of Twelve Shillings Value that he pay as a fine to ye King Ten Shillings & threeble damages for Said Corn to ye Said Peter being thirty Six Shilling & Costs & ffees & Stand Committed till Sentence be performed as p̄ the Sentence of the Said Justice Dated aprill 15th 1734 appears and now ye appelant appeared, to prosecute his appeal but an Exception being taken To the Reasons of appeal for that they were not properly Directed to the Court which Exception & ye pleas of Each party thereon being duly Considered The Court are of Opinion that ye Direction of the Said Reasons of appeal are Improper & Insufficient To Support the Same, Its therefore Considered by the Court, That the Sentence of ye Said Justice be Confirmed with additionall Cost vizt that the Said Ezekiell Upham pay as a fine to our Sovereign Lord the King The Sum of Ten Shillings that he pay to ye Said Peter Lawrance Threeble Damages for Said Two bushells of Corn being in ye whole thirty Six Shillings the Corn if any Return'd to be part thereof & pay Costs & ffees in the Taxed at the Sum of Seven pounds one Shillings & Seven pence and upon his neglecting to pay ye Same ye Court order Execution to be awarded for ye Same and that it be paid into ye hands of ye Clark to be by him paid To whom the Same is due.

˙Oliver Wallis of Worcester bound over by way of Recognizance as ℞ yᵉ Recognizance appeared his Recognizance was discharged

---

Thoˢ Gibbs & Moses Rice who were bound for yᵉ appearance of Jos Perey moved they might be discharge & were paying Cost as see yᵉ papers on file

---

A Petition of David Parsons of Leicester in yᵉ County of Worcester Cler' presented to this Court in Febry last & Continued to this Court, now Sitting Seting forth the great Inconveniencys & hardships he labours under by Reason of a Highway being laid as he apprehends Illegally a cross his lands in Leicester praying Relief as ℞ yᵉ petition will appear, at which Court he was directed to Serve yᵉ Town of Leicester &cᵗ & one John Lynds with a Copy of the Petition now to shew Cause why the prayer thereof Should not be granted & now all yᵉ partys appeared & after yᵉ Affair was fully debated and maturely Considered yᵉ petition was dismissed & yᵉ petitioner ordered to pay Cost which were done in yᵉ Court

---

A Petition of Paul Moore of Worcester housewright Sheweing that he together with Capᵗ Jonn Hubard of Worcester entered into a Contract with a Committee appointed by this Court for building yᵉ Court House which he has performed to good acceptance and doing which he has reely Expended about thirty or fourty pounds more yⁿ he Engaged yᵉ Same for as will appear by a schedule of Said work anexed to his petition praying allowance therefore as to yᵉ Court shall seem meet   Read & ordered that William Jenison John Chandler Jr. Henry [Lee] Esqʳˢ and Capᵗ Benjamin Flagg yᵉ Comittee for building Said house take said Petition and accoᵗ into yʳ Consideration & make report To this Court in august next what they may think proper for yᵉ Court to do thereon and that yᵉ Petition be Refered To that time

A By law of ye Town of Brookfield Respecting persons taking Cattle into Said Town &c^t presented by Col^o Dwight the Same was accordingly approved of and is on file

————

Dudley Jordan of a place called Lambstown in ye County of Worcester husbandman being presented by ye Grandjurors for unecessaryly rideing on ye Lords day being ye 28th day of October last past Came into Court and put himself on the mercy of ye Court and was dismissed paying Cost

————

David Aldriches two Recognizances Discharged about his absenting himself from ye Publick worship of God

————

David Aldrich of Uxbridge &c^t being presented to ye Court by the Grand jurors pleaded Guilty whereupon ye Court ordered that he pay a fine to ye King of fifty Shillings & Cost & fees & Stand Comitted till this Sentance is performed   which he paid and was dismissed.

————

Thomas adams of Worcester Husbandman and his wife Ruth Jessoniah Rice of Worcester Husbandman and Lydia his wife all came into Court & Severally acknowledged themselves Guilty of the Crime of fornication were fined to ye King Each Thirty Shillings which they paid with Cost & were dismissed

————

The Court order that for the future ye Clerk do not Signe or grant out any Sumonses for witnesses In Criminall Cases but what are directed to the Sheriff or his deputy or to a Constable to Serve & return

————

The Votes for a County Treasurer being Laid before ye Court Joseph Dwight Nahum Ward & John Chandler J^r Esqr were appointed a Comittee To Sort & number them and Report who is

Chosen attended yᵗ Service and Reported that Benjamin Flagg Jʳ was Chosen and yᵉ Oath of Office was accordingly administered To him by yᵉ Clark of yᵉ Court by order of & in yᵉ Court

———

Two orders or by laws of the Town of Worcester one Respecting Cattle and horses yᵉ other Rams were present for approbation & were accordingly approved

———

The Selectmen of mendon presented to yᵉ Court yᵉ warrant & warning of mary Thompson and also of Sarah Price with her Child all depart Said Town of mendon & are on file

———

The Selectmen of yᵉ Town of Worcester presented to yᵉ Court a warrant with yᵉ Constables return for warning Hanah Troy alˢ [   ] Margarett Troy to Depart their Town also a warrant with yᵉ Constables Return thereon for yᵉ warning David Smiley & Eliza Smiley depart their Town also a warrant with yᵉ Constables Return thereon for the warning an aged woman named Elizⁿ moore with her Two Sons Robert & Joseph moore and a young Child named Thomas Rodes all to Depart their Town praying the return thereof may be entered & approved which was done accordingly by yᵉ Court

———

The Court now order that yᵉ Comittee for yᵉ meeting house from time to time untill further order of the Court take Care To Keep yᵉ Court house in Repair that they do make Sutable ways to ascend yᵉ hill on which it Stands Clear the brush near the Same & lay their Charges from time to time before yᵉ Court for allowance

———

The Selectmen of yᵉ Town of Shrewsbury presented to yᵉ Court yᵉ warrant & warning of John Wilson & family To depart their Town and is on file

WORCESTER ss   *Anno R^i R^s Georgij Secundi nunc Magnæ Britaniæ Franciæ et Hiberniæ Octavo*

Att a Court of Generall Sessions of the peace begun and held at Worcester within and for the County-of Worcester on The Second Tuesday of August being the thirteenth day of Said month Annoq Dom 1734—

JUSTICES PRESENT

John Chandler Esqr	⎫ Justices of	Joseph Dwight Esqr
Joseph Wilder Esqr	⎪ ye Peace	Samuel Dudley Esqr
William Ward Esqr	⎬ &	Henry Lee Esqr
William Jenison Esqr	⎭ Quorum	Nahum Ward Esqr
Daniel Taft Esqr		Samuel Willard Esqr
John Chandler Esqr		John Keyes Esqr
Samuel Wright Esq		Edward Hartwell Esq
Jossiah Willard Esq		

CORONERS.

Captain James Wilder   Mr Joseph Wright

Mr Seth Chapin   Mr Gershom Rice

GRAND JURORS

Mr Joshua Child foreman	Mr Thomas Gleason
Mr Josiah White	Mr Benjamin Johnson
Mr Jotham Rice	Mr Daniel Warren
Mr Bazeliell Sawyer	Mr Isaac Amsden
Mr Jonathan Bugbee	Mr William Taylor

14

Capt Thomas Gilbert   Mr Eleazer Ball
Mr Joseph Sumner   Mr Nathan Heywood
Mr Ebenezer Read   N. B. Mr Simon Stone of
Mr Joseph Sibly   Harvard was Sick & did not attend
The Jury attended three days & an officer vizt with them

———

Peter Kendall of Lancaster In ye County of Worcester Labourer
being presented by the Grandjurors for ye body of Said County for
y^t he Said Peter Kendall at Lancaster aforesaid on or about the
midle of July 1733 did Comitt the Crime of Fornication on y^e body
of Beriah Knight of Lancaster aforesaid Spinster which is Contrary
to y^e peace of our Lord y^e King his Crown and dignity & y^e Good
& wholesome laws of this province as $\tilde{p}^l$ y^e presentment on file appears To which y^e Said Peter Kendall pleaded not Guilty and put
him Self on Tryall,   The Jury being Sworn according to law to
Trye y^e Case y^e Delinquent after a full hearing was Comitted To
y^e Jury who Return'd there verdict therein upon oath as follows
vizt that y^e Said Peter Kendall is Guilty in form aforesaid Its
Therefore Considered by The Court That the Said Peter Kendall
pay as a fine therefor to our Sovereign Lord ye King The Sum of
fifty Shillings & pay Costs & Fees Taxed at nine pound Seventeen
Shillings and Stand Comitted Till this Sentence be performed, at
which time the said Peter Kendall appealed To ye next Court of
Assize and Generall Goal Delivery to be holden at Worcester within and for ye County of Worcester on ye Wednesday Imediately
preceding the time by law appointed for holding ye Said Court of
Assize and Generall Goal delivery at Springfield within and for y^e
County of Hampshire In September next and Entered into Recognizance with Two Sufficient Suretys according to law To prosecute his appeal with Effect.
   Peter Kendall of Lancaster In ye County of Worcester Labourer
as principall In ye Sum of fourty pounds & Ralph Kendall Taylor
and Oliver Wilder Gent both of Lancaster In Said County as Suretys in Twenty pounds Each acknowledge themselves to be Indebted To our Sovereign Lord the King to be Leveyed on their
Severall goods Chattells lands & Tenaments and in want thereof

on their bodys for ye use of our Said Lord ye King his heirs or Successors Conditioned that ye Said Peter Kendall prosecute his appeal To Effect at ye Said Court of Assize & Generall Goal delivery To be holden in & for Said County of Worcester and abide ye Judgment of said Court & not Depart without Leave and in the mean time be & Remain of ye Good behaviour

---

Beriah Knight of Lancaster Single Woman being presented by the Grandjurors for her being Guilty of ye Crime of Fornication came into Court Confessed herself Guilty was find thirty Shillings which She paid & was Dismissed

---

John Brown of Watertown &c^t being presented by ye Grand Jurors for his Unecessaryly Rideing on ye 28th day of aprill last past being ye Lords day came into Court & pleaded To ye Insufficiency of ye presentment for y^t he has not his addition properly given him was Dismissed paying Cost wch he paid

---

Megee Dupee of Lancaster being presented by the Grandjurors for being Guilty of the Crime of Fornication & bound over To answer for ye Same by m^r Justice Wilder appeared and pleaded She was not bound to answer ye Same She not having her right name The Court Considered ye Same & She was Dismissed paying Cost wch she paid.

Thomas Currier and John Damon being presented by ye Grandjurors for Rideing Unecessaryly on ye Lords day as ₽ ye presentment appeared and pleaded they were under a necesaty of rideing ye Court order y^t yy be dismissed paying Cost wch were paid

---

William Gray Junr & Sam^ll Gray both of Worcester being Severally presented by ye Grand Jurors for being Guilty of drunkenness appeared before ye Court & Severally pleaded Guilty to their presentments were each find five Shillings to ye use of ye poor of ye Town of Worcester & to pay Costs wch they paid & were dismissed

Ephraim Smith of Shrewsbury & Hari^n his wife both being presented by ye Grandjurors for being Guilty of ye Crime of Fornication came into Court and Confessed them Selves Severally Guilty were find Each To ye King thirty Shillings & to pay Cost which they paid & were dismissed

Daniel Hill Husbandman & Nath^ll Emerson Cordwainer both of Mendon being presented by ye Grandjurors &ct as ꝑ ye presentment appears for Rideing Unecessaryly on ye third day of Febry last past &ct being ye Lords day came into Court & pleaded Guilty were fin'd Each thirty Shilling To the poor of ye Town of mendon & to pay Cost — paid

Meriam Jones wife of Daniel Jones of Brookfield Came into Court & Confessed that She was Guilty of ye Crime of Fornication was fin'd thirty Shillings & Dismissed paying Cost

Nath^ll Bartlett of Brookfield Confest himself Guilty of ye Crime of Fornication was Sentenced to pay a fine of thirty Shillings & Cost which he p^d & was Dismissed

The Town of Southborough being presented for not having a writing & reading Schoolmaster &ct by their Selectmen & were dismissed paying Cost

Solomon Johnsons Petition Dismissed

Jane Morss wife of Sam¹ Morss of Uxbridge &c̄t being presented for her Unecessaryly absenting herself from y͏ᵉ publick Worship of God as ꝑ y͏ᵉ presentment appeared & put her Self on y͏ᵉ mercy of y͏ᵉ Court, was dismissed paying Cost

---

Peter Kendall & Hepzibah his wife of Lancaster appeared in Court and Confessed yᵐselves Guilty of fornication were find Each thirty Shillings & dismissed paying Cost

---

The Select men of y͏ᵉ Town of Woodstock presented a warrant with their Constables Return for warning on Wᵐ Russell & his wife to leave their town wᶜʰ was approved by y͏ᵉ Court

---

William Peirce of Westborough in y͏ᵉ County of Worcester husbandman upon y͏ᵉ Complaint of Asher Rice of Sᵈ Southborough to Nahum Ward Esq was by him bound over to this Court as ꝑ y͏ᵉ Recognizance and Complaint appears   The affair was laid before the Grandjury who upon a bill prepared by y͏ᵉ Kings attorney Return'd y͏ᵉ Same Ignoramus whereupon y͏ᵉ Court dismissed y͏ᵉ affair & Each party bore his own Cost

---

Eliphalett Warfield of Mendon In y͏ᵉ County of Worcester was bound over to this Court by Danˡˡ Taft Esqr to answer to his presentment by the Grandjury for Unecessaryly labouring on a public fast &c̄t as ꝑ y͏ᵉ presentment pleaded to y͏ᵉ Insufficiency of y͏ᵉ Same and was ordered to be dismissed pay Cost Taxed at five pound & Ten pence wᶜʰ he refuseing to do was ꝑ order of Court Comited to his majestys Goal there to remain till dismissed by order of law

John Hamilton of Shrewsbury in the County of Worcester Labourer appearing in Court To answer to his presentment by y[e]
Grandjurors for that he the Said John Hamilton at Worcester In
y[e] County of Worcester on y[e] fourteenth day of august Instant in
y[e] night time did feloniously take and Steel out of y[e] Pockett of
Samuel Lawdy of medfield in y[e] County of Suffolk Gent about
four or five pound in bills of Creditt with Some papers being y[e]
proper Estate of y[e] Said Lawdy all which is against y[e] peace of
our Said Lord y[e] King his Crown and dignity and y[e] good and
wholsome Laws of this province as p̃ y[e] presentment on file To
which y[e] Def[n] pleaded not Guilty and put himself on Tryall by a
Jury who were Sworn to Try y[e] Same y[e] Deft having been fully
heard y[e] Jury went out to Consider thereof & Return'd there verdict Therein finding y[e] Def[n] [Joseph Crosby not Guilty][1]

Its Considered by y[e] Court that y[e] Defend[t] be Dismissed paying Cost & ffees Taxed at five pound & Tenpence Standing Comitted Till Sentence be performed

————

Ezekiell Upham of Hassanamisco in y[e] County of Worcester
Housewright appel[t] from a Sentence given against him by Nahum
Ward Esq[r] one of his majestys Jus[s] of y[e] peace for said County on
y[e] Complaint of Peter Lawrence of Said Hassanamisco Indian
planter for stealing Corn &c̃ as p̃ y[e] Sentence of Said Justice on
file, (This Tryal now being by order of y[e] Great & Gen[ll] Court)
& now y[e] Def[n] pleaded not Guilty & put himself on Tryall by a
Jury who were Sworn to try y[e] Same y[e] Deft having been fully
heard y[e] Jury went out to Consider thereof & Return'd there Verdict therein finding y[e] Def[n] not Guilty Its therefore Considered by
the Court That y[e] Said Ezekiel upham be dismissed paying Cost
& ffees Taxed at five pound 18/ & Sixpence and upon his neglecting To pay y[e] Same The Court order Execution To be granted
therefor and y[t] it be paid into y[e] hands of y[e] Clerk of the Court To
be paid To whom it is due

———————

[1] Words in brackets cancelled.

John Fitz Gerald al' John Hayes al' John m'neal a Transient person now Resident in Worcester In said County appearing in Court To answer to his presentment by y* grandjurors for y' he on or about the 29 day of July last past at medfield in the County of Suffolk did then and there feloniously take Steal and Carry away fifty pounds in bills of Creditt and merchants notes and Six Silk handkerchiefs of the Vallue of Ten Shillings Each being y* proper Estate and then in the possession of Samuel Lawdy of medfield aforesaid Gent and did also Continue the Said theft at Worcester in y* Said County of Worcester by concealing the said bills of Creditt notes and Handkercheifs all w*¹ is highly Criminall and agaiust y* peace of our Said Lord the King his Crown & Dignity and y* Good and wholsom Laws of this province as p̃ y* presentment To which y* Def¹¹ pleaded not Guilty & put himself on Tryall by a Jury who were Sworn to Trye y* Same The Def¹¹ having been fully heard The Jury went out to Consider thereof and Return'd there Verdict therein finding y* Def¹¹ Guilty

Its Considered by the Court that the Said John Fitz Gerall al' John Hays al' John m'neal be whipt on y* naked body Twenty Stripes That he pay the Said Samuell Lawdy threeble y* mony & goods Stole viz' one hundred & fifty nine pounds The mony & goods found To be part thereof, and upon his neglecting to pay y* Same That he be bound To y* S^d Sam¹¹ Lawdy his heirs and assigns At Ten pounds p̃ year to pay y* Same that he pay Cost & fees taxed at fourteen pounds nine Shillings & Six pence and Stand Comitted till Sentence be performed

[Worcester ss august 18 : 1731 Capt Lawdy rec^d fifty one pound fifteen shillings & nine pence besides paying y* Cost 14 : 9 : 6 att' Jn° Chandler Jr Cler]¹

Abraham Anderson of Harvard In y* County of Worcester husbandman appearing in Court To answer to his presentment by y* Grandjurors for that the Said Abraham Anderson at a place Called

¹ Sentence in brackets written on the margin.

Concord in Harvard aforesaid on or about the Twenty first day of
May last past did feloniously Take Steal and drive away a Certain
Cow being the Proper Estate of Hekekiah Wheeler of Concord in
ye County of Midlesex Yeoman and in his Yard & possession then
being which is against the peace of our Said Lord The King his
Crown & Dignity and ye Good and wholsom laws of this province
as p̃ ye presentment on file To which ye Def^t pleaded not Guilty
& put himself on Tryall by a Jury who were Sworn To Trye y^e
Same, The Deft being fuly heard The Jury went out To Consider
thereof and Returned there Verdict thereon finding ye Deff^t Guilty,
Its Considered by the Court that the Said Abraham Anderson pay
as a fine To our Lord ye King ye Sum of fifty Shillings   That He
pay To ye Said Hezekiah Wheeler Eighteen pounds be[ing] threeble ye Vallue of the Cow said Cow if return'd to be part and pay
Cost & fees & Stand Comitted till this Sentence be performed

The Court order that the Committee for building the Court house
alter the Jury Seats So as that they will Comfortable Hold the
Jurys and that they make Sutable ways for going To ye Court house
ye Charge to be laid before ye Court for their attendance

The Court order that the Charge of ye Search after one Thomas
Peirce who had murdered a person on Rhoad Island be paid To
William Jenison & John Chandler J^r Esq to be by y^m paid to whom
it [is] due

Tavern Keepers and Retailors

Lycenced ye year Ensuing & y^t gave bond

Worcester

Capt Haywood
Moses Rice
Thos Starns } Inholders
Gershom Rice Jr }
John Bigelow
Lieutt Davis

Lancaster

Capt Carter
Mr Wm Richardson
Mr Josiah Richardson
Mr Jonathan Houghton
                Inholders
Colo Saml Willard retailer

Mendon

Capt Wm Rawson
Mr Ebenr Mencon
Mr John Sadler Inholders
Capt Lovett retailor

Woodstock

Capt Jona Payton
Mr Joseph Wright
            Inholders

Brookfield

Mr Moses Leonard
Mr Elea: Heywood
Mr Solomon Keyes
            Inholders

Leicester

Capt Converse
Mr Thomas Richardson
Mr Jona Sargent }
Mr Rowland Taylor } Inholders
Mr Wm Larkin retailor

Hassanamisco

Capt Leland
Capt Willard } Inholders
James Cuttler }
Nehe : How

Uxbridge

Mr Ezekiel Wood
Mr Solomon Wood
Mr Saml Read Inholders
Mr Jno Harwood retailor

Oxford

Elijah Moore Inholdr

Shrewsbury

Mr Daniel How
Mr John Burts Inholders
Nahum Ward Esqr
Mr Jonas Keyes retailors

Westboro'

Capt Jno Fay Inholder

Southborogh

Mr Robert Horn
Mr Caleb Witherbee
            Inholds

Lunenburg

Capt Jona Hubbard
            Inholder
Colo Josiah Willard
            retailor

Harvard

Mr John Atherton
Mr Ebenr Robins
            Inholders
Mr Ebr Sprague
            Retailor

Sutton

Mr Perez Rice
Mr Obediah Walker
Mr Jno Hazeltine
            Inholders
Capt Elisha Johnson
Mr Wm Hartwell
            retailor

New Sherborn

Mr Eph Hill
            Inholder

Dudley

Mr Danl Coburn

Rutland

Capt John Hubbard

In all 53

Capt Philip Goss approbated
but no bond given

15

NOTE.

LICENSE LAW. The following act regulating the sale of spirituous liquors was in force at this time :

" An Act for the suppressing of Unlicensed Houses, and the due Regulation of such as are, or shall be Licensed.

"Be it ordained and Enacted by the Governour, Council and Representatives convened in General Court, and by the Authority of the same. That no Person or Persons whatsoever (other than such as upon producing Certificate from the Select-men of the Town where they dwell or who shall be otherwise thought fit by the Justices themselves, shall be licensed by the Justices in Quarter Sessions) may presume to be a common victualler, Innholder, Taverner, or Seller of Wine, Beer, Ale, Cyder, or Strong Liquors by Retail: nor shall any presume without such License, to sell Wine or strong Liquors privately by a less Quantity than a Quarter Cask, and that delivered and carried away all at one time ; on pain of forfeiting the Sum of *Forty Shillings* for every such offence, upon due Conviction thereof ; one Half thereof to the Informer, and the other Half to the Use of the Poor of the Town where such offence is committed. . . . . . .

" Be it further enacted by the Authority aforesaid, That all Licences be renewed yearly, and the Bond given for the due observance of the same and of the Laws; and that the Person licensed shall use his License in such Houses as shall be therein named, and no other."

If the offender refused or was unable to pay his fine, he was publicly whipped.

Att a Court of Generall Sessions of the peace begun and held at Worcester within and for the County of Worcester on The first Tuesday of November being the fifth day of Said month Annoq Dominij 1734—

JUSTICES PRESENT

Joseph Wilder, William Ward & William Jenison Esq^{rs} Justices of the Peace & Quorum — John Chandler J^r Edward Hartwell Henry Lee,, Nahum Ward and Samuell Willard Esq^{rs} Justices

———

NAMES OF CORONERS

Capt James Wilder   Mr Seth Chapin J^r Mr Joseph Wright
Mr Gershom Rice

———

Mr Joshua Childs Mr Josiah White Mr Bazeliell Sawyer Mr Jonathan Bugbee Mr Joseph Sumner Mr Eben^r Read Mr Joseph Sibley Mr Benjamin Johnson Mr Daniel Warren Mr Isaac Amsden Mr William Taylor Mr Eleazer Ball Mr Nathan Heywood Mr Jotham Rice   Each 2 days & Richard Wilds attended on them

Hannah Dankin being bound over to this Court by m^r Justice Jenison To answer to her Crime of fornication appeared in Court & Confessed she was Guilty, She was Sentenced to pay a fine of thirty Shillings & Cost which She did & was dismissed

———

The Town of Lunenburg being presented by ye Grandjurors for not having a writing & Reading Schoolmaster agreeable to law appeared & were Excused paying Costs

———

John Wallis of Townsend in ye County of Midlesex husbandman being presented by the Grandjurors for his Unecessaryly Traveling on ye Lords Day &c^t appeared and gave his Reasons & was Excused

———

The wife of Nathaniell Bartlett of Brookfield in ye County of Worcester appeared in Court & Confessed She was Guilty of the Crime of Fornication was find Thirty Shillings & paid Costs & was Dismissed

———

John Dunsmore & wives Recog' Continued To Feb'y
Nath^{ll} Davenport & wives Recognizance continued To Feb'y
Benj^a Chaffee Recognizance Continued To Feb'y
Town Leicesters presentment continued to Feb'y

———

A Petition John Harwood agent for ye Town of Uxbridge Seting forth the great Burden & Difficulty ye Said Town labour under Respecting ye Charge of building Bridges in said Town as more particularly appears by ye Petition praying for relief Read & Refered to ye Court of Generall Sessions of ye peace in Feb^r next for further Consideration & ordered that the petitioner Serve ye Town of Mendon with a Copy thereof that they Shew Cause if any they have why ye prayer thereof Respecting mendon Should not be granted

WORCESTER ss *Anno R^i R^s Georgij Secundi nunc Magnæ Britainiæ Franciæ et Hiberniæ Octavo*

At a Court of Generall Sessions of the Peace begun and Held at Worcester within and for the
County of Worcester on the first Tuesday of
February being the fourth day of Said Month
annoq Dom : 1734-5

John Chandler   ⎫   Joseph Dwight   ⎫
Joseph Wilder   ⎪ Esq^{rs} Justices of   Samuel Dudley   ⎪
William Ward   ⎬ ye peace & Quo'   Henry Lee   ⎬ Esq^{rs}
William Jenison   ⎭   Nahum Ward   ⎪
                                        John Keyes   ⎪
Daniel Taft   ⎫   Edward Hartwell ⎭
                   ⎬ Esq^{rs}
John Chandler Jr   ⎭

Names of Coroners Capt James Wilder   Mr Joseph Wright
                   Mr Seth Chapin   Mr Gershom Rice

Grandjury y^t attended

Capt Daniel Warrin   Mr Eben^r Read   Mr William Taylor
Mr Josiah White   Mr Joseph Sibley   Mr Eleazer Ball
Mr Jotham Rice   Mr Thomas Gleason
Mr Bazeliell Sawyer   Mr Benjamin Johnson
Mr Jonathan Bugbee   Mr Isaac Amsden   Mr Nathan Heywood
                                          Mr Simon Stone

Mr Wilds attended on y^m & they attended Two days Each

Tabitha Bellows of Southborough appeared in Court and Confessed She was Guilty of the Crime of fornication by one Benony Salter, for which she paid a fine of thirty Shillings & was Dismissed paying Cost also Mary Latiney of Westborough Single Woman came into Court & Confessed She was Guilty of the Crime of Fornication with one Thomas Dooley find Thirty Shillings & dismissed without Costs

---

Nathaniel Davenport of Woodstock & Elizabeth his wife being presented by the Grandjurors for the Crime of Fornication   The Said Nathaniel appeared and Confess'd the Same & paid a fine of fifty Shillings & Cost & was dismissed his wife not being able To attend her Recognizance was continued to may

---

John Dunsmore of Lancaster & Unice his wife being presented by the Grandjury for ye Crime of Fornication came into Court & plead To ye Insufficiency of the presentment which was by the Court adjudged Insufficient & they were Dismist paying Costs

---

The Court now order that a Tax or assessment amounting unto the Sum of One hundred & fifty Seven pound Eight Shillings & nine pence be ra'sed in the Severall Towns within this County for defraying ye usuall necessary Charges ariseing within ye Same and that the Clerk forthwith Send out Warrants directed To ye Selectmen or assessors of the Respective Towns within ye County for assessing their Severall parts or proportion according to ye Rules for assessing ye last province Tax as ye law directs and for paying in ye Same To Capt Benjamin Flagg County Treasurer or his order at or before ye last day of may next—

The Severall Towns proportion thereof is as follows vizt

Worcester Eleven pound Seven Shillings & Eight pence	11	7	8
Lancaster Twenty Six pound three Shillings & four pence	26	3	4
Mendon Eighteen pound	18		
Woodstock Sixteen pound	16		
Brookfield thirteen pound Ten Shillings & 8d	13	10	8
Southborouh Eight pound thirteen Shillings	8	13	
Westborough nine pound one Shilling	9	1	
Leicester Six pound nineteen Shillings & Eight pence	6	19	8
Shrewsbury Seven pound Seven Shillings	7	7	
Sutton Twelve pound five Shillings	12	5	
Oxford Seven pound Two Shillings	7	2	
Uxbridge Six pound & four pence	6	0	4
Rutland three pound Eighteen Shillings	3	18	
Lunenburg three pound Eighteen Shillings	3	18	
Harvard Seven pound three Shillings & one peny	7	3	1
	157	8	9

the Warrants were Granted out Febry 8th 1734

att^s Jno Chandler J Cler^t

Ordered that The Sum of Six pounds be paid out of ye County Treasury To William Jenison Esqr for Inlarging ye Prison Yard laying a double floor in ye Prison Chamber

---

An acco^tt of Mr Sheriff Gookin amounting unto ye Sum of Sixteen pound Seven Shillings Read and ordered that the Sum of fifteen pound nine Shillings be paid out of ye County Treasury To Mr Sheriff Gookin in full discharge thereof Nineteen Shillings Taken out of ye 5th article

---

David Parsons of Leicester in the County of Worcester Clark appellan^tt from a Sentence given against him by William Jenison Esqr one of his majestys Justices of the Peace for the Said County

DOM REX

v^s

PARSONS

JURY

Mr James Taylor
Mesr R: Flagg
Mr Eb: Beman
Joseph Walker
John Moss
Henry King
Elisha Hedge
Tim: Brigham
Aaron Forbush
Wells Ayres
Wm Haywood
Israel Keith

upon a Complaint of Benjamin Johnson of Leicester aforesaid Yeoman on His majestys behalf as well as of his own (which Complaint was originally made to John Chandler J^r Esqr one of his majestys Justices of the peace for said County) against the appel^{lt} Seting forth y^t ye Said David Parsons at Leicester aforsaid on the Seventh day of October last past did very much abuse misuse belye and Defame the Coplainant by Saying ye Complain^t was a Tatling man or a Tatler and went about from House to House Raising Factions (meaning as the Complainant Supposes against him Said Parsons) and by Saying that the Complainant had Stolen Two years Sallary from him Said Parsons Intending thereby as ye Complain^{tt} apprehends to very much abuse misuse belye & defame ye Complain^t &c^t as ẜ ye Complaint at large appears, and was thereof Convicted before the Said William Jenison Esqr & Sentenced to pay a fine to the King Ten Shillings and pay all Costs & Fees & Stand Comitted till Sentence be performed—and now the appellant appeared and to the Said Complaint Pleaded not Guilty ; The Evidences in the Case being Sworn and the Case fully Argued and heard on both Sides the Same was Comitted To the Jury who were Sworn according to law to Trye ye Same and Return'd there Verdict therein upon Oath as follows vizt, That the Said David Parsons Is Guilty according to the Complaint   Its therefore Considered by the Court that the Said David Parsons Pay as a fine To our Sovereign Lord the King for and Towards the Support of the Goverm^t of this Province and the Incident Charges thereof Ten Shillings and that he pay Cost & Fees Taxed at fifteen pound one Shilling, & Stand Comitted Till Sentence be performed, & he was accordingly Comitted To Mr Sheriff Gookin till the Sentence be complyed with

———

A Complaint of John Overing Esqr his majestys attorney General for the province of the Massachusetts in behalf of our Said Lord ye King Seting forth that one James Orns was convicted before the Worshipfull Justice Joseph Dwight Esqr. upon a Complaint Exhibitted at the Instance of Seth Banister & Francis his wife for speaking Defamatory words of ye Said Francis of which he was Convict then & there & ordered to pay ye Sum of Twenty Shillings as a fine (from which sentence he appealed & found Suretys for his good behaviour) & pay Costs & fees To this Hon^n Court butt having faild to prosecute to Effect prays affirmation &ct To which ye Said Orms pleaded that there was not a Sufficient time from ye Sentence given agst him, To the Court appealed To for him to file his reasons of appeal & moved The whole proceeding might be Quash'd Its Considered by the Court That there was not a Sutable time agreeable To law between ye giving of the Sentence & ye Court appeald to whereby ye Said Orms Could seasonably file his reasons of appeal & therefore order he be dismiss'd paying Cost & fees Taxed at Eight pounds & Two pence and upon his Neglecting to pay ye Same ye Court order Execution to be awarded for ye Same   Ex : March 1 : 1734/5

———

Samuell Morss of Uxbridge Recognizances Discharged

Benjamin Chaffee of Woodstock Recognizances Discharged ye woman & Child being Dead

———

A Petition of John Harwood agent for the Town of Uxbridge prefered To the Court of Genl Sessions of the Peace held In November last Came under Consideration as also the answer of ye Town of Mendon by their agent or attorney & ye Same being Duly Considered ordered that said Petition be Dismissed

———

The Select men of Worcester presented to the Court a warrant with a Return thereon by Wm Gray J^r Constable for warning Sundry persons out of their Town   also a warrant with a Return thereon by Joseph Rug a Constable for warning Sundry persons out of their Town both which were approved by the Court

16

The Select men of Shrewsbury presented to the Court Two warrants one for Warning Josiah Pratt & his wife The other Phillip Gleason & his wife to depart Said Town with the Constables Return Thereon which were accepted by the Court.

An acco⁴ Signed John Chandler Jʳ amounting To the Sum of Ten pound Eleven Shillings & Sixpence ariseing on acco⁴ of yᵉ Charge of pursuing & Searching after Thomas Peirce who had murdered a person at New : port   Read & ordered that the Sum of Ten pound Eleven Shillings & Sixpence be paid out of the Publick Treasury of yᵉ County To John Chandler Jʳ Esqʳ To be by him paid To whom the Same is Respectively due in full discharge thereof

---

Mathew Barber of Shrewsbury in the County of Worcester Husbandman being Presented by the Grandjurors for the body of said County on their Oaths for unecessaryly Traveling on the Lords day in the month of October last from Shrewsbury To Worcester in Said County and Bound over to this Court by way of Recognizance To answer To his presentment appeared in Court and Confessed he was Guilty of Rideing from Shrewsbury to Worcester The time mentioned in the presentment, but Justifyed his So doing because his Rideing was Only from his own House To a place of Publick Worship in Worcester where he found by Experience Twas most for his Spirituall advantage to attend   The Case being duly Considered, The Court are of opinion that the Said Mathew Barber is Guilty of unecessaryly Traveling as set forth in yᵉ presentment and therefore adjudge that he pay as a fine the Sum of Thirty Shillings, vizt fifteen Shillings part thereof to be for the benefitt & Relief of yᵉ Poor of the Town of Shrewsbury and fifteen Shillings Part thereof to be for the benefitt & Relief of yᵉ Poor of the Town of Worcester, and pay Cost & Fees Taxed at one pound fifteen Shillings & nine pence from which Sentence The Said Mathew Barber appealed To the next Court of Assize and Generall Goal Delivery to be holden at Worcester in and for the County of Worcester in September next and Entered into Recognizance pursuant to law to prosecute his appeal with Effect

Mathew Barber of Shrewsbury In the County of Worcester husbandman principall In the Sum of Ten pounds and Robert Barber Clothier and Hugh Kelso husbandman both of Worcester In ye County aforesaid as Suretys in five pounds Each acknowledged themselves bound by way of Recognizance To our Sovereign Lord the King his heirs or Successors To be Leveyed on their Goods or Chattels lands or Tenements for the use of our Said Lord the King Conditioned that the Said Mathew Barber shal personaly appear at S^d Court of Assize & prosecute his appeal aforesaid apeal with Effect & in the mean time be of the good behaviour.

A By law of the Town of oxford Respecting persons takeing in Cattle or horses into Said Town under a penalty &ct being presented by Captain Ebenezer Learned was allowed and approved off and is on file

----

Capt Samuel Lawdy Representing to this Court That a Certain Double Silk Gown a black Silk apron & Scarf, which goods found with John Fitz : Gerald al' John Hayes al' John m^cneal who had Stollen a Considerable Quantity of mony & goods from him and of which he was Convicted in august last, are now in the hands of Daniell Gookin Esqr. Sheriff of this County and were ordered there to Remain till the further order of this Court, moving that pursuant to the Judgment of Court he may have ye goods aforementioned in part of Satisfaction of Said Judgment Especially Since the S^d Fitz Gerald &ct Broke Goal & Run away. Ordered that Said Double Silk Gown black apron & Scarf be delivered to Said Capt Samuel Lawdy or his order and John Chandler J^r Esqr is desired to appoint & put under oath three Sutable persons to apprize Said Goods, and that Said Lawdy Receive them at Said apprizement in part of Satisfaction for Said Judgment of Court

att^r   John Chandler J^r Cle.

May 13th : 1735   the above Goods were apprized & delivered To Capt Lawdy   See his Rec^t in Sessions affairs for may 1735

WORCESTER ss *Anno Regni Regis Georgij Secundi nunc Magnæ Britaniæ Franciæ et Hiberniæ Octavo*

Att a Court of Generall Sessions of the Peace begun and held at Worcester within and for the County of Worcester on The Second Tuesday of May being the thirteenth day of Said month Anno Dom: 1735

JUSTICES PRESENT

John Chandler	⎫	John Chandler Jr	⎫
Joseph Wilder	⎬ Esqrs Justices of	Samuel Wright	⎬
William Ward	⎱ ye peace & Quo'	Joseph Dwight	⎱ Esqrs
William Jenison	⎭	Samuel Dudley	⎭

Henry Lee
Nahum Ward
John Keyes

———

Coroners   Capt James Wilder   Mr Seth Chapin Jr
Mr Joseph Wright   Mr Gershom Rice

———

Grandjurors: Names

Mr Joshua Child foreman

Mr Josiah White	Mr Ebenr Read	Mr Eleazer Ball
Mr Jotham Rice	Mr Joseph Sibley	Mr Nathan Heywood
Mr Bazeleel Sawyer	Mr Thomas Gleason	Mr Simon Stone
Mr Jonathan Bugbee	Mr Benjamin Warrin	
Capt Thomas Gilbert	Mr Isaac Amsden	Mr Benja Johnson
	Mr William Taylor	

Each attended Two days and Mr Wilds attended them

New Jury were

Mr Jonathan Houghton foreman

Mr Joseph Crosby   Mr Wm Ayres   Mr James Heaton

Mr John Starnes   Mr William Green Mr Thomas Hapgood

Mr Isaac Thayer   Capt Daniel Taylor Mr William Jones

Mr Eliphalett Carpenter Mr John Stock   Mr Caleb Sawyer

Mr William Ayres   Mr Gershom Keith Capt John Fay

They were Sworn & Dismissed

Capt Benjamin Flagg County Treasurer presented his acco^ts^ which were Examined and allowed of ⅌ the Court there being due to the Treasurer Twenty one Shillings and four pence and ordered the Clerk to Sign the Same

----

Bemsley Peters of Woodstock In ye County of Worcester Felt-maker appeared Court & also Han^a^ his wife & Confessed they were Guilty of the Crime of Fornication before marriage were fin'd 30/ Each & ordered to pay Cost which was done & they were Dismissed

----

Elizabeth Davenport wife of Nathaniel Davenport of Woodstock In the County of Worcester husbandman being bound over by John Chandler Esqr to answer for the Crime of Fornication appeared in Court & Confessed She was Guilty, was find fifty Shillings & to pay Costs which She did & was Dismissed

----

Joseph Baxter of Uxbridge In the County of Worcester Cord-wainer being bound over by way of Recognizance To answer for the Crime of Fornication appeared in Court and Confess'd him Self Guilty was find thirty Shillings wch he paid with the Costs & was Dismissed

The Selectmen of Woodstock presented to the Court a warrant directed to Joseph Childs one of their Constables to warn one Susanna Carter To depart there town with the Constables Return thereon which was approved by the Court

---

William Wait of Sutton in the County of Worcester husbandman being presented by the Grandjurors for that on or about the 16th day of January last past at Sutton aforesaid he with force & arms an assault on ye body of Joseph Wait in ye peace of our Lord the King did Comitt, &c appeared in Court & pleaded Guilty and have himself on the mercy of the Court & Shew'd himself very penitent Its therefore Considered by the Court that the Said William Wait pay a fine of Ten Shillings to our Lord ye King That he pay Costs & fees Taxed at Two pound Thirteen Shillings and upon his neglecting So to do The Court order Execution To be awarded for the Same

---

A Petition of Isaac Tomlin of Westborough &c presented to ye Court praying yt ye Children & Grand Children of his mother in law Ruhamah Wait widow may be obliged to Contribute towards ye maintainance of ye Said Widdow, Read and ordered that the Petitioner Serve ye Children and Grand Children (whose proper ancestor is Decd) of the Sd Ruhamah Wait with a Copy of this Petition that So they Show Cause if any they have at ye next Court of Genl Sessions of the Peace to be held here on the Second Tuesday of august next vizt on the first Thursday of the Courts Seting why they Should not be assessed according to law towards the Support and maintainance of ye Said Ruhamah Wait

---

An accot of the Grandjurors Travell and attendance from may 1734 To may 1736 being presented amounting unto ye Sum of of Seventy Eight pounds Eight Shillings & Eight pence allowed of by the Court and The Treasurer is accordingly ordered To pay the Same

The vote for a County Treas.' Sent in from the Several Towns were opened & Sorted in the Court and it appeared that Cap.' Benj.ª Flagg was Chosen Unanimously & the oath of office was admin'stred to him In Court by The order of the Court

WORCESTER ss *Anno R¹ Rˢ Georgij Secundi nunc Magnæ Britainiæ Franciæ et Hiberniæ Nono*

At a Court of Generall Sessions of the Peace begun and Held at Worcester in and for the County of Worcester on the Second Tuesday of August being the Twelfth day of Said Month annoq Dom 1735

JUSTICES PRESENT

John Chandler Esqʳ	} Justices of the peace & Quorum	Samuel Wright	
Joseph Wilder Esqʳ		Joseph Dwight	
William Ward Esqʳ		Samuel Dudley	} Esqʳˢ
William Jenison Esqʳ		Henry Lee	
Daniel Taft Esqʳ		Nahum Ward	
John Chandler Jr Esqʳ		Samˡ Willard	

John Keyes } Esqʳˢ
Edward Hartwell

Coroners Present Capt James Wilder   Mʳ Joseph Wright
             Mʳ Edward Godard Junʳ   Mʳ Gershom Rice

Grandjury

Mʳ Jonᵃ Houghton	Mʳ William Ayres	Mʳ James Heaton
Mʳ Joseph Crosby	Mʳ Will: Green	Mʳ Thomas Hapgood
Mʳ John Starnes	Capᵗ Danˡ Taylor	Mʳ William Jones
Mʳ Isaac Learned	Mʳ John Stockwell	Mʳ Caleb Sawyer
Mʳ Isaac Thayer	Mʳ Gershom Keith	attended three day and
Mʳ Eliphalett Carpenter Capᵗ John Fay Mʳ Wilds attended on them		

Benjamin Bullard of Lancaster &c being bound to appear at this Court To answer for the Crime of Fornication with Ruth his wife before marriage Came into Court & Confes'd ye Same was fined thirty Shillings & dismissed paying Cost : *his wife bond Cont*[d]

The Select men of mendon presented to ye Court a warr[t] for warning Jane Pollen To depart their Town with ye Constables Return thereon ; accepted by ye Court

---

A list of Tavern Keepers and Retailors Lycenced by this Court & ye names of the Suretys

Worcester
{ Capt Daniel Heywood principall in 50/: Capt Benja Flagg & James Moore Gents Suretys 25/ Each
Capt Moses Rice Ditto 50/   Capt Flag & John Harwood Suretys. 25/ Each
Mr Thomas Starnes Do 50/   Capt Flagg & Daniel Ward Suretys 25/ Each
Mr Simon Davis Do 50/   John Bigelow & Caleb Witherbee Southboro' Suretys Ditto
Mr John Bigelow Ditto 50/   Simon Davis & Caleb Wither Do }

Lancaster
{ Capt Thomas Carter   } Mr Jona Houghton of Lancaster
Capt William Richardson) was Principall for Each of them
Mr Josiah Richardson   ) in 50/ Each and Capt Jonas
Mr Jona Houghton   ) Houghton & Elias Sawyer of Lancaster Suretys for Each in 25/ Each
Mr Benja: Houghton: Principall: Suretys Capt Jonas Houghton & Henry Lee Esqr
Saml Willard Esqr Retailor: Edward Hartwell Esqr his principall Suretys Ephraim Witherbee and Fairbank Moore }

Mendon
{ Capt William Rawson principall Surety Jno Sadler of upton & Jno atherton of Harvard
Mr Ebenr Merriam Do) Suretys for Each other & John Sad-
Capt Daniel Lovett Do } Retailor }   ler for them both }

Woodstock
} Capt Jonathan Payson | Capt Flag principall for Each in 50/
} Mr Joseph Wright | Henry Lee and Edward Hartwell Esqrs Suretys for Each in 25/

Brookfield
Mr Eleazer Heywood principall: 50/: Suretys Jonas Keyes & Israel Richardson
Mr Soloman Keyes: Jonas Keyes principall Suretys Isrel Richardson & Elea' Heywood
Mr Nathll Read principall Colo Dwight & Capt Flagg

Oxford
Mr Elijah Moore: Capt Moore principall. Suretys Capt Flagg & Joe: Crosby
Mr Moses Marcy principall—Suretys Capt Flagg & Jno Stacy New Medfield

Sutton
Mr Perez Rice Samuel Dudley Esqr: principall, 50/ Suretys Joseph Boyden Wm Stockwell
Mr Obadiah Walker, principall: Suretys Capt Wm Rawson John Atherton
Mr Joseph Boyden principall Suretys Samuel Dudley Esqr Wm Stockwell
Mr William Stockwell Retailor principall Suretys Saml Dudley Esq Joseph Boyden

Rutland
Capt John Hubbard principall Suretys James Heaton Nathll Read

Southboro'
Mr Robert Horn principall, Suretys Jno Harwood Epm Hill
Mr Caleb Witherby principall Suretys Simon Davis John Bigelow

Leicester
Mr Thomas Richardson principall Suretys Henry Lee Esqr Eleazer Heywood
Capt Josiah Convers principall Mr Wm Larkin Capt Benja Flagg
Mr Jona Sargent principall: Suretys Isaac Richardson Eleazer Heywood
Mr Wm Larkin Retailor: principall Suretys Capt Convers & Capt Flagg

Uxbridge
Mr Ezekiel Wood
Mr Solomon Wood } Each principall & bound one for
Mr Samuel Read } another
Mr John Harwood principall Suretys Robert Horn Ephraim Hill
Mr Benja Force Jno Harwood principall: Suretys Mr Edmd Goffe als Trowbridge of Cambridge and Mr Isaac Coolidge of Sherborn both in ye County of Midlesex

Lunenburg
Mr Ephraim Witherbee principall: Suretys Edwd Hartwell Esqr Fairbanks Moore
Mr Isaac Farnsworth
Josiah Willard Esqr. Edwd Hartwell principall Suretys Ep: Witherbee Fairbanks Moore

Grafton
Capt James Leland
Capt Samuel Willard } Each principall and bound for each
Mr Nehemiah How } other

Dudley — Mr Daniel Coburn principall: Suretys Jno Harwood Richard Wilds

Shrewsbury —
} Capt Daniel How: Nahum Ward Esqr principall Suretys Capt Flagg & Jno Harwood
Mr John Bush principall Surety Jona Sargent & Jno Harwood
Nahum Ward Esqr Retair: principall Suretys Capt Flagg & Jno Harwood
Mr Jonas Keyes Retair: principall. Suretys Eb: Heywood & Israel Richardson

Westborough — Capt John Fay Do Suretys Wm Stockwell & Samuel Dudley Esqr

Upton —
} Mr John Sadler } Each principall & Each Surety for ye
Mr John Hazeltine } other: & Ebenezer Merriam for both.

Harvard —
Mr John Atherton principall Surety Capt Wm Rawson & John Sadler
Mr Eleazer Robins Do Suretys Capt Jonas Houghton Eleazer Sawyer
Mr Ebenr Sprague Retair: Do Suretys Jno Atherton & Jno Bush

New Medfield — Mr John Stacy Do Suretys Joshua Morss & Moses Marvin

New Sherborn — Mr Ephraim Hill Do Suretys John Harwood & Robert Horn

Lambstown — Mr Nathan Carpenter Do Surety John Frissell & David Wallis

Each principall bound in fifty pound & Each Surety in Twenty five pounds Each

The Selectmen of Worcester presented to ye Court Sundry Warrants directed to their Constables for warning persons out of their
Town vizt on to Constable Daniel Biglo To warn James Culver to
depart the Town one To ye Same Constable To warn Joshua Wheat
& family To depart there Town one To ye Same Constable to warn
Wm Campbell & James Bettys To depart ye Town all which being
done as p̃ ye Constables Return, they were approved of by ye Court

---

Robert Allen of Shrewsbury being bound over To this Court by
way of Recognizance by Wm Jenison Esqr as p̃ ye Recog' appears
moved to be Discharged, but Sundry persons appearing and oposed
it The Court order that he Renew his bonds with Suretys untill
the Next Term which he Did vizt himself in Fifty pound & Sam^ll
Calhoon of S^d Shrewsbury and James Furbus of Worcester as Suretys in Twenty five pounds

---

Abigail Willard of Lancaster In ye County of Worcester Singlewoman being bound over To this Court by Mr Justice Hartwell for
the Crime of Fornication appeared and Refuseing to Tell who y^e
father was She was Sentenced To pay a fine of fifty Shillings & Cost
& Fees & Stand Comitted till Sentence be performed—which She
paid in Court and by ye order of Court Entered into Recognizance
with Suretys To Save ye Town of Lancaster from any Charge on
acco^tt of her Bastard Child vizt The Said Abigail Willard as principall in One hundred pound & Aaron Willard & Fairbanks moore
both of Said Lancaster Yeomen as Suretys in fifty pound Each to
ye Select men of Lancaster aforesaid, & to their Successors for that
purposs.

Whereas its found very Inconvenient To ye County For ye Court
of Generall Sessions of the Peace and Inferiour Court of Comon
pleas which by law are appointed to be held and Kept on the
Second Tuesday of August yearly by reason its Then a very busy
time of year and thereby Detrimentall for Jurors & Others who

have business at Said Courts to give their attendance. Ordered That the Hon⠀Joseph Wilder Esqr John Chandler Jʳ & Joseph Dwight Esqrs be desired in the name and by order of this Court To prefer a Petition To his Excellency The Govʳ & The Genᶫᶫ Court as Soon as they Conveniently can To have the time for holding Said Court for the future to be on the third Tuesday of August annually, and Whereas it might be of Service To yᵉ County to have the time for holding yᵉ Court of Assize & Genᶫᶫ Goal De·livery & Superior Court of Judicature which by law is now holden on the Wednesday Imediately preceeding the time appointed for holding Said Court at Springfield in and for the County of Hampshire The Said persons are desired To Consult The Honᶫᶫ His majestys Justices of yᶜ Said Court of assize &c̄t for their advice what other time may be more accomodable for holding the Same & if they then shall think it proper that they Prefer a Petition accordingly

— —— —

A Petition of Isaac Tomlin as Entered at the Last Term, being duly Served on the Children & Grand-Children of yᵉ Widdow Ruhamah Wait, and all yᵉ partys now appearing and fully heard thereupon The Court order that the Cost & Charge which the Said Isaac Tomlin hath hirtherto been at in the Support of the Said Ruhamah Wait and his Charges & Cost in prefering his Petition &c̄t amounting unto the Sum of Twelve pound Two Shillings be paid as follows Wᵐ Wait & Joseph Wait of Sutton Two of yᵉ Sons of yᵉ Said Widdow Each Three pound & Six pence David Joss Joshua Josiah Kesiah & martha newton Grandchildren of yᵉ Said Widow Each Ten Shillings & one peney & that the Remaining three pound & Sixpence be born by the Said Isaac Tomlin, & Nathaniel Pratt of Framingham who maryed a daughter of yᵉ Said Widdow being uncapable to Labour and unable To pay Towards her Support is freed therefrom till yᵉ further order of this Court

And the Court further order that Dureing the time the Said Ruhamah Wait Shall board at yᶜ Said Isaac Tomlins, That The Said William Wait Pay towards her Support Till yᶜ further order of this

Court one Shilling & three pence ℔ week the Said Joseph Wait pay yᵉ like Sum of one Shilling & three pence ℔ week and that the Said David Joss Joshua Josiah Kesiah & martha Newton pay Each of them one peny half peny ℔ week & that the Same be paid Quarterly unto the Said Isaac Tomlin and upon their Neglect Respectively of making payment of the Sums aforesaid They Forfeit Twenty Shillings apeice ℔ month agreeable to law To be Leveyed & Imployed as ℔ yᵉ Law for that end is appointed

----

An accoᵗ of John Chandler Jʳ Esqr procureing Cushings &ᶜᵗ amounting unto Seven pound one Shilling & Sixpence allowed & the Treasurer of the County is ordered to pay yᵉ Same accordingly

----

William Jenison Esqr Informing this Court that the Inhabitants of the Town of Grafton[1] formerly Called Hassanamisco neglect & Refuse to pay their part or proportion of the Charge of laying out The County Road from Worcester To Mendon being three pound Six Shillings The Court Therefore order the Clerk To Send forth an Execution or Warrant of Distress agᵗ The Select men or Some other principall person of Said Town of Grafton for Said Sum

Then yᵉ Court was adjourned to Thursday yᵉ 21 : Instant 9 o'Clock forenoon

----

[1] Incorporated as a town in 1735.

WORCESTER ss *Anno R^i R^s Georgij Secundi nunc Magnæ Britainiæ Franciæ et Hiberniæ &c Nono*

At a Court of Generall Sessions of the Peace held at Worcester by adjournment on Thursday the 21st day of August, Annoq Dom: 1735

JUSTICES PRESENT

John Chandler	John Chandler J^r	Samuel Willard Esq
Joseph Wilder) Esqs	Josiah Willard) Esqrs	
William Ward)	Nahum Ward)	
William Jenison	Henry Lee	John Keyes Esqr

––––––

The Court agreed To present the following Congratulatory address To His Excellency Jonathan Belcher Esqr, Capt Gen^{ll} and Governour in Chief in and over His Majestys Province of ye Massachusetts Bay in New England now in the Town of Worcester

May It Please your Excellency.—We his majestys Justices of the Court of Generall Sessions of the Peace now held In this place for the County of Worcester by adjournm^t, humbly beg leave to Congratulate your Excellencys Safe arrivall in this part of your Government—It is with hearts full of Joy that we now See your Excellencys face together with the Hon^{ll} Councill in the Shire Town of this County which has Rec^d its being and Constitution by ye favour of your Excellency under ye Divine Conduct and Benediction, and by whose wise, mild and Just administration, this whole Province enjoys great Quietness, which we Trust will be Continued and accepted in all places, with all thankfulness, We are also Sensibly affected that your Excellency has Condescended and is now pursuing a very necessary (altho a very Difficult and Tedious) Journey to visitt the Western Frontiers & meet with the Cagnawaga Indians and Such Tribes as may be desireous to renew their friendships with this Government in order to preserve and perpetuate the happy Peace Subsisting with them—may your Excellency and the Honourable Gent of the Councill and Such of the Hon^ll House of Representatives who attend you, be encompassed with the Divine favour as with a shield and in due time return'd in Safty to your Respective Habitations

Worcester August 21 : 1735   which was Read To his Excellency by the Honbl John Chandler Esqr first Justice of the peace in the County, To which his Excellency was pleas'd to Return the following answer——

Gent I thank you very Kindly for ye welcome you give me with ye Honll Gent of his majestys Councill and the Gent of ye House of Representatives into this part of his majestys province ; I take this opportunity of assureing you that I shall always Cheerfully Joyn my power with yours that Justice and Judgment may flourish in the County of Worcester which will greatly Contribute to the Happiness and welfare of the People

after which the Justices of Said Court Return'd to ye Court house and the Court was adjourned without day

---

NOTE.

Jonathan Belcher was governor of Massachusetts from 1730 to 1741. He was born in Cambridge in 1682, and graduated at Harvard College in 1699. While on a visit to Europe he formed an acquaintance with the Princess Sophia and her son, afterwards George I.; and to this circumstance he was indebted for his future honors. His administration in Massachusetts was creditable; and he maintained his popularity until his removal, which was accomplished through the intrigues of certain parties whose schemes he had opposed. Appointed governor of New Jersey in 1747, he died in office ten years later.

Governor Belcher visited Worcester again in 1740, in company with White-field, the celebrated preacher.

At a Court of Generall Sessions of the Peace begun and held at Worcester in and for the County of Worcester on the first Tuesday of November being the fourth day of Said Month anno : Dom : 1735

JUSTICES PRESENT

John Chandler Esqr	⎫ Justices of	John Chandler Jr Esqr
Joseph Wilder Esqr	⎬ the Peace	Nahum Ward Esqr
William Ward Esqr	⎨ & Quorum	Samuel Willard Esqr
William Jenison Esqr	⎭	John Keyes Esqr
		Justices of the Peace

———

Grandjury

Mr Jonathan Houghton foreman

Mr Joseph Crosby	Mr Wm Green	Capt Danl Taylor
Mr John Haines	Mr John Stockwell	Mr William Jones
Mr Isaac Learned	Mr Gershom Keith	Mr Caleb Sawyer
Mr Eliphalett Carpenter	Capt John Fay	Mr James Heaton
	Mr Thomas Hapgood	

Each attd three days & Mr Wilds attend ym

———

David Young of Worcester within ye County of Worcester husbandman being presented by ye Grandjurors for ye County aforesd

18

YOUNG D JURY

Mr Thos: Pratt
Will: Nicolls
Epm: Wilder Jr
Maturin Allard
Simeon Maynard
John Gibbs
Caleb Barton
Jon Hobs
Jno Sanderson
Simon Davis
Wm Brown
Timo: Carter

for his Unecessaryly Travelling at Rutland and Worcester in ye County aforesaid on the last Lords Day before the presentment, as ₱ ye presentment appears was bound by way of Recognizance To appear at the Court of Generall Sessions of the Peace held on the Second Tuesday of August last past, at which Court Said Recognizance was Continued to this Court and now the Said David Young appeared and pleaded not Guilty upon which plea ye Case after a full hearing was Comitted to the Jury who were Sworn according To Law to Try ye Same and Returned their Verdict therein upon Oath as follows vizt that the Said David Young is Guilty, Its therefore Considered by the Court That the Said David Young Pay as a fine to the Selectmen or overseers of the Town of Rutland for ye Use of the Poor of the Said Town thirty Shillings, that he pay Costs & Fees, Taxed at Six pound four Shilling and Stand Comitted till Sentence is performed which he Refuseing to pay was Comitted according

---

The Selectmen of Worcester presented a warrant directed to one of their Constables To warn John Partrick his wife and family to depart their Town and it being duly served, its accordingly approved of by ye Court

---

The Court now order that a Tax or assessment amounting unto the Sum of one hundred and fifty Seven pound Eight Shillings & nine pence be raised on the Severall Towns within this County for defraying the usuall necessary Charges ariseing within the Same and that the Clark forthwith Send out Warrants directed to the Selectmen or assessors of the Respective Towns within ye County for assessing their Severall Parts & proportions according to the Rules for assessing the last province Tax and for paying in ye Same to Capt Benjamin Flagg County Treasurer or To his Successors at or before the last day of may next.

The Severall Towns Proportion thereof is as follows viz'

Worcester	Eleven pound Seven Shillings & Eight pence	11	7	8
Lancaster	Twenty Six pound three Shillings & four pence	26	3	4
Mendon	fifteen pound fourteen Shillings	15	14	
Woodstock	Sixteen pound	16		
Brookfield	Thirteen pound Ten Shillings & Eight pence	13	10	8
Southboro'	Eight pound thirteen Shillings	8	13	
Westborough	Nine pound one Shilling	9	1	
Leicester	Six pound nineteen Shillings & Eight pence	6	19	8
Shrewsbury	Seven pound Seven Shilling	7	7	
Sutton	Eleven pound five Shilling	11	5	
Oxford	Seven pound Two Shillings	7	2	
Uxbridge	Six pound & four pence	6	0	4
Rutland	three pound Eighteen Shillings	3	18	
Lunenburg	three pound Eighteen Shillings	3	18	
Harvard	Seven pound three Shillings & one peny	7	3	1
Upton	Three pound Six Shillings	3	6	0
	Sum Total	157	8	9

Warrants were Issued out Nov^r: 11th 1735
att^s Jno. Chandler J^r Cl

An acco^t of Daniel Gookin Esqr Sheriff of ye County amounting unto Seventeen pound thirteen Shillings & four pence   Read and ordered That the Sum of Seventeen pound thirteen Shillings & four pence be paid out of the County Treasury in full discharge thereof to the Said Mr Sheriff Gookin in full Discharge thereof

---

An acco^tt of John Chandler J^r Esq amounting unto Seven pound Sixteen Shillings   Read and allowed and order'd that the Said Sum of Seven pound Sixteen Shillings be paid out of the County Treasury to the Said accomptant in full discharge thereof.—This aco^t is withdrawn after it pas'd

---

Betty Houghton being bound by way of Recognizance To appear at this Court To answer To the Crime of fornication, Did not appear but forfieted her bond which was Ten pound which was paid in Court

-----

Allexander McClure's Recognizance Discharged paying Cost of Court wch was p^d

John McJerald's Recognizance Discharged pay Cost. p^d

Robert Hunters Sam^{ll} Dunkins & Robert Allens Recognizance discharged

Mary Barbers recognizance at her husbands request Continued to february she not being well

-----

Nathaniel Sawyer of Lancaster In the County of Worcester husbandman and Mary his wife being bound by way of Recognizance to appear at this Court to answer to the Crime of Fornication appeared & Confess'd the same were fin'd Each thirty Shilling & Costs wch they paid & were dismissed

-----

Simon Stone of Shrewsbury Husbandman & Easter his wife and his Son Daniel Stone al being presented by ye Grand Jury for Unecessaryly absenting themselves from the Publick Worship of God &c^t appeared & gave their Reasons and were Excused paying Costs which were paid

-----

Experience Bartlett of Brookfield Spinster being bound to appear at this Court To answer for the Crime of Fornication appeared & Confessed the fact but not being delivered Her bonds were Continued To the next Term

-----

Joseph Doolittle of Kingstown in the County of Hampshire now Resident in Brookfield in ye County of Worcester husbandman being bound by way of Recognizance To appear at this Court To answer To a Complaint made agst him by Experience Bartlett of of Said Brookfield Spinster for his begitting her with Child by fornication and she not bein yet delivered The Court order That he Renew his Bonds Namely him Self in the Sum of one hundred pound & Two Suretys in fifty pound Each for his appearing at the next Term and abideing ye Order of Court & not to depart without lycence.

——————

Thomas Mackintire of Rutland In the County of Worcester husbandman being presented by ye Grandjurors for Said County for y^t on ye 25th day of Augs^t 1734 being Sabath day he did wilfully and unecessaryly presume to Travell from Rutland aforesaid To Worcester in ye County of Worcester aforesaid being the Space of Twelve miles as ℘ the presentment appears The said Thomas McKintire was brot before ye Court and Confess'd he Did Travell as Set forth in ye presentment but Said it was not Unecessary Travell; and being fully heard thereon The Court Judge the Said Thomas McKintire is Guilty of Unecessary Travell as set forth in ye presentm^t: and therefore Sentence ye Said Thomas McKintire to pay a fine of thirty Shillings to the Selectmen or overseers of ye Poor of the Town of Worces for the use of ye Poor of Said Town That he pay Cost & fees Taxed at four pound Eleven Shillings & Stand Comitted Till Sentence is performed.—and he Refuseing to pay the Same was Comitted accordingly

Novr. 12 : 1735 he paid ye fine & Costs & was accordingly Discharged

——————

John Slarah of Rutland in the County of Worcester husbandman being presented by the Grandjurors for said County for that on ye 25th day of August 1734 being Sabath day he did wilfully and unnecessaryly presume to Travell from Rutland aforesaid to Worcester In ye County of Worcester afores^d being the Space of Twelve miles &c as ℘ ye presentment appears The Said John Slarrah was brought before the Court and Confess'd he did Travell as set forth In the presentment but said it was not unecessary Travell and fully heard thereon The Court Judge the said John Slarrah is Guilty of unecessary Travell as set forth In ye present and therefore order that the said John Slarrah pay a fine of thirty Shillings to the Selectmen or overseers of the poor of the Town of Worcester for the use of the Poor of Said Town that he pay Cost & fees Taxed at four pound Sixteen Shillings and Stand Comitted till Sentence is performed and he refuseing to pay ye Same was Comitted accordingly

Novr 12 1735   he paid ye fine & Costs & was Discharged

———

Andrew McClain of Rutland In ye County of Worcester husbandman being present by the Grand Jurors for said County for that on the 25th day of august 1735 being Sabath day he did wilfully and Unecessaryly Travell from Rutland aforesaid To Worcester In ye County of Worcester aforesaid being the Space of Twelve miles &c as p ye presentment appears   The said Andrew McClain came into Court and Confess'd he did Travell as set forth in the presentment but said it was not Unecessary Travell and being fully heard thereon The Court Judge The Said Andrew McClain is Guilty of Unecessary Travell as Set forth in the presentm^t and therefore Sentence the Said Andrew McClain [to] pay a fine of thirty Shillings To the Selectmen or overseers of ye Poor of ye Town of Worcester for ye Use of Said Poor that he pay Cost & Fees Taxed at Three pound Eleven Shillings and Stand Comitted till Sentence is performed, and he Refusing to pay ye Same was accordingly Comitted, Novr. 12 : 1735 he p^d ye Same & was discharged

———

Thomas Ward of Westborough In ye County of Worcester husbandman being bound by way of Recognizance with Suretys To appear at this Court To answer To his presentment by the Grand Jurors for his willfully & Unnecessaryly neglecting to attend the Publick worship of God on Lords days for more than one month last past before ye presentment as p ye presentment appears, appeared in Court and pleaded not Guilty, The Case after a full

D Ris. T. WARD
JURY

Tho: Pratt
Mr Wm Nicolls
Epm Wilder Jr
Maturin Allard
Simeon Maynard
Caleb Barton
Jno Gibbs
Jona Hobs
Jno Sanderson
Simon Davis
Wm Brown
Tim: Carter

hearing was Comitted to ye Jury who were Sworn according to law to Trye ye Same & Return'd there Verdict therein upon [oath] as follows vizt that the Said Thomas Ward is Guilty Its therefore Considered by ye Court That the Said Thomas Ward pay a fine of Twenty Shillings To the Selectmen or overseers of ye Poor of ye Town of Westborough for ye use of the poor of said Town That he pay Costs & Fees Taxed at Two pound Two Shillings & four pence and Stand Comitted Till Sentence be performed, From which Sentence ye Said Thomas Ward appealed To the next Court of assize and Generall Goal Delivery to be holden at Worcester within and for the County of Worcester In September next and Entered into Recognizance with Suretys according To law for prosecuting his appeal with Effect &c^t vizt Thomas Ward of Westborough Husbandman Benjamin Flagg J^r of Worcester Gent & John Harwood of Uxbridge Joyner all in the County of Worcester appeared before ye Court and acknowledged themselves bound by way of Recognizance vizt The Said Thomas Ward as principall in Twenty pound and the Said Benjamin Flagg J^r & John Harwood as Suretys in Ten pound Each To our Sovereign Lord the King his heirs or Successors to be Leveyed on their Goods or Chattells lands or Tenaments for ye Use of our Said Lord ye King &c Conditioned That if the Said Thomas Ward Shall personally appear at Said Court of assize and Gen^ll Goal Delivery and Shall prosecute Said appeal with Effect and Shall do and perform what Shall by Said Court be Injoyn'd him & not depart without Lycence & in the mean time be of the good behaviour then said Recognizance To be void Else To abide in full force and Virtue—Sepr 6. 1736 Mr Tho: Ward paid the fine & Cost att^e Jno Chandler J^r Cl

Thomas Ward of Westborough In ye County of Worcester husbandman being bound by way of Recognizance with Suretys to appear at this Court To answer to his presentment by the Grand Jurors in nov^r 1734 for his wilfully & Unnecessaryly neglecting to

DOM REX
vs
TH WARD

Same Jury as: 1st: case

attend the Publick Worship of God on Lords days for more than one month last past before yᵉ presentment as ⅌ yᵉ Same appears appeared in Court and pleaded not Guilty, The Case after a full hearing was Comitted to the Jury who were Sworn according to law to Trye yᵉ Same and Returned there Verdict there in upon [oath] as follows vizᵗ That the said Thomas Ward is Guilty Its therefore Considered by the Court That the Said Thomas Ward pay a fine of Twenty Shillings to the Selectmen or overseers of yᵉ Poor of the Town of Westborough for the use of the Poor of Said Town that he pay Cost & Fees Taxed at Two pound Two Shillings & four pence and Stand Comitted Till Sentence be performed

From which Sentence The said Thoˢ Ward appealed To the next Court of assize and Generall Goal Delivery to be holden at Worcester in and for the County of Worcester in September next and entered into Recognizance with Suretys according to law for prosecuting his appeal with Effect &ct as follows vizᵗ The said Thomas Ward as principall In the Sum of Twenty pound and Benjamin Flagg Jʳ of Worcester Gent and John Harwood of Uxbridge Joyner both in the County of Worcester as Suretys in Ten pounds Each personally appearing before the Court and acknowledged themselves bound by way of Recognizance In yᵉ aforesaid Sums Respectively to our Sovereign Lord the King his heirs or Successors To be Leveyed upon their Goods or Chattells lands or Tenemtˢ for the Use of our Said Lord yᵉ King &ct Conditioned that If the Said Thomas Ward Shall personally appear at Said Court of Assize and Generall Goal Delivery and Shall prosecute Said appeal with Effect and Shall doe and perform what by Said Court Shall be Injoyned him and not Depart without Lycence and in the mean time be of yᵉ Good behaviour Then said Recognizance to be void Else to abide In full force & virtue

Sepr 6. 1736 Mʳ Tho Ward paid yᵉ fine & Cost

attˢ Jnⁿ Chandler Jʳ Cl

WORCESTER SS *Anno R¹ R³ Georgij Secundi nunc Magnæ Britainiæ Franciæ et Hiberniæ Nono*

At a Court of Generall Sessions of the Peace begun and Held at Worcester in and for the County of Worcester on the first Tuesday of Febry being the third day of Said Month anno Dom 1735-6

JUSTICES PRESENT

John Chandler ⎫
Joseph Wilder ⎪ Esqrs Justices
William Ward ⎬ of the Peace
William Jenison ⎭ & Quorum

Sam¹¹ Wright Esqʳ
Samuel Dudley Esqʳ
Henry Lee Esqʳ ⎫ Justices
Nahum Ward Esqʳ ⎬ of the
Samuel Ward Esqʳ ⎭ Peace
John Keyes Esqʳ

Daniel Taft ⎫ Esqrs
John Chandler Jʳ ⎭

Grand Jury

Mʳ Jonᵃ Houghton foreman

Mʳ Joseph Crosby	Mʳ Wᵐ Green	Mʳ Caleb Sawyer
Mʳ John Starnes	Mʳ Dan¹ Taylor	Mʳ Isaac Thayer
Mʳ Isaac Learned	Mʳ John Stockwell	Mʳ William Ayres
Mʳ Eliphalett Carpenter	Mʳ Gershom Keith	Mʳ James Heaton
Mʳ Thomas Hapgood	Capᵗ John Fay	Mʳ William Jones

Mʳ Richard Wilds Depᵗ Sheriff attended them

19

Stephen Chapman of Woodstock &ct bound over to this Court for Breach of Peace appeared acknowledged The fact was find five Shillings & to Pay Costs which he did and was Dismissed

---

The Selectmen of Worcester presented a Warrant directed to one of their Constables To warn one Thomas Green his wife & family To depart their Town and it being duly Serv'd its approved

---

Isaac Coller Oliver Coller & Lydia Coller all of them being presented for not attending on ye Publick Worship of God &ct all of them appeared and pleaded their poverty & not living within any Town, and promising as soon as they could to Reform were dismiss'd

---

Thomas Ward of Westborough &ct being presented for his unecessaryly Traveling on ye Lords [day] &ct appeared & made his Excuse & was dismissed paying Costs

---

Joseph Sanouse an Indian being presented for Unecessaryly Traveling on ye Lords day &ct appeared & made his Excuse & was dismiss'd paying Cost

---

Mathew Barber of Shrewsbury being presented for Unecessaryly Traveling on the Lords day &ct appeared & made his Excuse & was dismᵈ paying Cost

---

Mary Barber wife of Mathew Barber being presented for Unecessaryly Traveling on the Lords [day] Sepʳ. 14 : 1735 appeared & made her Excuse & was Dismissed paying Cost

Robert M⁽Cain of Rutland being presented for Unecessaryly Travelling on yᵉ 25ᵗʰ of Aug: 1734 appeared and made his Excuse and was dismis⁽ᵈ⁾ paying Cost

———

The Town of Brookfield being presented for want of a Bridge over Marks River &c appeared and assured the Court they would speedily build yᵉ Same were dism⁽ᵈ⁾ paying Cost

———

The Court now order that for the future Wednesday yᵉ Second day of the Courts Siting being at the Severall Courts hereafter held in November and Feb'y be Sessions days and thursday the third day of the Courts Siting at the Severall Courts hereafter held in may & august be Sessions days.

———

The Court order that a well be dug on the Prison ground or as near the Same as may be at the Charge of the County & William Jenison John Chandler J⁽ʳ⁾ & Henry Lee Esq⁽ʳˢ⁾ & M⁽ʳ⁾ Sheriff Gookin are desired to fix yᵉ place for yᵉ Same & See it dug & well Stone on as Easy Terms as may be

———

This Court order that a Cart Bridge be Erected and built at the Charge of the County over a River Called French River between Worcester & Oxford at or near the place where yᵉ present Road Crosses Said River it being not in any Town & there being great need of a Bridge there and to be from time to time Repaired at the Charge of the County till the Court Shall order otherwise & Cap⁽ᵗ⁾ Benjamin Flagg and M⁽ʳ⁾ Gershom Rice Jun⁽ʳ⁾ are appointed a Comittee To Se yᵉ Same Effected and then to lay their acco⁽ᵗ⁾ before yᵉ Court for their approbation & allowance

———

Joseph Doolittle and Experience Bartlett being bound over to this Court by M⁽ʳ⁾ Jno Dwite To appear at the last Term as appears by their Respective Recognizances were then again Bound to appear this Court & now they appeared and Confess'd they were Guilty of yᵉ Crime of fornication were find Each thirty Shillings & Cost and were dism^d

----

John Rich Junr of Dudley &ct being bound To appear at this Court by the Hon^l John Chandler Esqr To answer to a Charge Exhibitted against him &ct as ₱ yᵉ Recognizance appears Came into Court & promising Reformation of what was amiss in him was dismiss'd.

The Selectmen of Grafton presenting a warrant directed by them to the Constable of Grafton To warn John Ward his wife & family & nath^ll Whitemore his wife & family to depart there Town &ct it was ordered to be put on file

----

DOM REX
vs
PARSONS

David Parsons of Leicester in yᵉ County of Worcester Clerk being presented by the Grand Jurors for said County for that yᵉ said David Parsons at the meeting House in Leicester aforesaid on the Twentyth day of aprill last past it being the Lords day Did then and there make a Disturbance in the Publick worship of God by words and actions &ct as ₱ the presentment fully and at large appears, was bound by way of Recognizance with suretys to appear at the Court of Generall Sessions of the Peace held at Worcester the first day of November last past at which Court Mr Parsons appeared and at his desire the Case was Continued to this Term & now yᵉ Said Parsons appeared and pray'd the presentment might be Quas'd as ₱ his pleas on file appear Which were over-Ruled by the Court & to the presentment or Crime alledged pleaded not Guilty, Upon which plea the Case after a full hearing was Comitted to the Jury who were Sworn according to law to Trye yᵉ Same and Return'd their Verdict therein upon oath vizt That the said David Parsons is Guilty Its therefore Considered by the Court that the said David Parsons pay as a fine to our Sovereign Lord the [King] as a fine twenty five Shillings That he pay Cost & Fees & Stand Comitted till Sentence is perform'd, he paid ye fine & Cost in Court & was dismiss'd

———

William M^carry of Wrentham In ye County of Suffolk Husbandman being presented by the Grandjurors of our Lord ye King for the County of Worcester for that ye Said William on or about the Twenty ninth day of December last past at a place called Boston in the Township of Worcester in ye County of Worcester afores^d at the House of Mrs Maylems did take Steal and Carry away a pockett Book or mony Case wherein was one pound five Shillings & Sixpence in paper Bills and in bonds and notes of hand and accounts to ye Vallue of Sixty or Seventy pounds and of the proper Goods or Estate of one John Salisbury of Bristoll in ye County of Bristoll Inholder alwhich is highly Criminall and ag^t the peace of our Sovereign Lord the King &c^t The Deft appeared & pleaded not Guilty The Case after a full hearing was Comitted to the Jury who were Sworn according to law to Trye ye Same and Return'd there Verdict therein upon oath as follows vizt that the Said William M^Carry is not Guilty Its therefore Considered by ye Court that the Said William M^Carry be Dismiss'd paying Cost

WORCESTER SS *Anno Regni Regis Georgi Secundi nunc Magnæ Britaniæ Franciæ et Hiberniæ Nono* ⌒

Att a Court of Generall Sessions of the Peace begun and Held at Worcester in and for the County of Worcester on the Second Tuesday of May being the 11th day of Said Month anno Dominij 1736

JUSTICES PRESENT

John Chandler Esqr
Joseph Wilder Esqr
William Ward Esqr   } Justices of
William Jenison Esqr   { the Peace
John Chandler J^r Esqr   } and Quo-
                           rum

Samuel Dudley ⎫ Esqrs
Henry Lee   ⎬ Justices
Nahum Ward   ⎭ of the Peace

———

Coroners Capt James Wilder Mr Seth Chapin J^r Mr Joseph Wright & Mr Gershom Rice

———

Old Grand Jury

Mr Jon^a Houghton foreman

Mr Joseph Crosby	Capt Daniel Taylor	Mr James Heaton
Mr John Starns	Mr William Green	Mr Thomas Hapgood
Mr Isaac Thayer	Capt John Fay	Mr Caleb Sawyer
Mr Eliphalett Carpenter	Mr Gershom Keith	Mr William Jones
Mr William Ayres	Mr Isaac Learned	Mr John Stockwell

Mr Richard Wilds Dep^t Sheriff attended on them

New Grand Jury for 1736

Sutton   Mr Robert Goddard foreman
Worcester   Mr Thomas Rice   Mr Nath^ll Green Leicester
            Mr Cyprian Stevens Mr Jon^a Furbush Westboro'
Mendon   Mr Nathan Tyler   Mr Joseph Taft Junr Uxbridge
Woodstock   Mr Joseph Lyon   Rutland Mr James Wright
Brookfield   Mr John Ayre   Lunenburge Mr Benjamin
Mr David Fay Southborough   Goodrich
Mr Symon Maynard Shrewsbury   Harvard Mr John Daly
Mr Samuel Davis Oxford   Grafton Mr James Whiple
            Lancaster Mr Elias Sawyer

They were Sworn & Sent home

David Farnsworth and Hanah his wife both of Lunenburg &ct
came into Court and Confessd themselves Guilty of the Crime of
fornication were find thirty Shillings Each and Cost & then dism^d

------

Sarah Bucknum of Sutton ·Singlewoman came into Court & Confess'd she had been Guilty of ye Crime of fornication was find
thirty Shillings & Cost & then dismiss'd.

James Magregore of Grafton &ct being presented by the Grand
jury for Unecessary Traveling on the Lords day made his Excuse
and was dismissd paying Costs

The Select men of Mendon presented a warrant directed to
their Constable to warn Mary Thoits to depart their Town & being
duly Served was approved

An acco^t of John Chandler J^r Esqr amounting unto the Sum of
of fourteen pound Six Shillings allowed of by the Court and the
County Treasurer is accordingly order to pay ye Same

Benjamin Flagg County Treasurer presented his accounts from may 1735 To May 1736. which were Carefully Examined by the Court and accordingly approved of the ballance in favour of the County when all yᵉ Taxes are paid is fifty Three pounds fourteen Shillings & Ten pence & the Court direct the Clark to Signe yᵉ Same in yᵉ name of yᵉ Court

---

The Votes Sent in from the Several Towns in the County for the Choice of Register of Deeds were opened in & Sorted [by] the Court. The Number of Votes wer 522 : and it appeared that John Chandler Jʳ Esqr was Elected by 517 Votes and was accordingly Sworn to the faithfull discharge of his office by the Honⁿ Joseph Wilder Esqr

---

The Votes Sent in from yᵉ Several Towns for yᵉ Choice of a County Treasurer being opened & Sorted by yᵉ Court it appeared that there were Two hundred Sixty Eight Votes and that Capᵗ Benjamin Flagg was Elected by 266. votes and was according Sworn to yᵉ faithfull discharge of his office by yᵉ Clerk in & by order of the Court

---

A By law of the Town of Lunenburg prohibiting Cattle & Horses from being brought into their Town &ct was presented to the Court and according allowed of and approved by the Court

---

A Petition of Nathaniel Dike & nine others Inhabitants of Sutton Seting forth the Great Difficulty they Labour under for want of a Sutable Road from Sutton to Worcester the Shire Town of yᵉ County Read & ordered that William Jenison Esq Major Jonas Rice and Capᵗ Benjamin Flagg be a Comittee to Consider of Said Petition as to the necessaty of a Road being laid out and to view and make Report as Soon as may be To this Court of what they may think proper to be done In answer to Said Petition

WORCESTER SS *Anno R¹ R⁸ Georgij Secundi nunc Magnæ Britainiæ Franciæ et Hiberniæ Decimo*

Att a Court of Generall Sessions of the Peace begun and Held at Worcester within and for the County of Worcester on the Second Tuesday of August being the Tenth day of Said Month annoq Dominij 1736

John Chandler   Esqrs   Josiah Willard Esqʳ
Joseph Wilder   ⎫ Justices of   Nahum Ward Esqʳ
William Ward   ⎬ the Peace   Joseph Dwight Esqʳ
William Jenison   ⎭ and Quo-
                  rum   Samˡˡ Willard Esqʳ
John Chandler Jʳ   Samuel Dudley Esqʳ
   Henry Lee Esqʳ   Edward Hartwell Esqʳ   John Keyes Esqʳ
                   Justices of the Peace

———

Capt James Wilder   Mʳ Seth Chapin Jʳ   Mʳ Joseph Wright & Mʳ Gershom Rice Coroners

———

Grandjury

Mʳ Robert Goddard foreman

	Mʳ David Fay	Mʳ Symon Maynard
Mʳ Thomas Rice	Mʳ Nathˡˡ Green	Mʳ Benjᵃ Goodrich
Mʳ Cyprian Stevens	Mʳ Jonᵃ Furbush	Mʳ John Daly
Mʳ Elias Sawyer	Mʳ Joseph Taft	Mʳ James Whiple
Mʳ Nathan Tyler	Mʳ Samˡˡ Davis	Each attᵈ Three days and
Mʳ Joseph Lyon	Mʳ James Wright	Mʳ Isaac Farnsworth
	Depᵗ Sheriff attended on them	

The Court Taking into Consideration the small Extent of the
Prison yard, and Mr Jotham Rice the under Keeper of the Prison
who has got a Dweling House & land adjoining thereto being will-
ing to Subject it for that use The Court therefore order the Prison
yard be Inlarged vizt on ye Side next the County Road To Extend
Southerly on ye Same Course ye Yard now is so far as That a line
Extending westward as said Rices fence now Stands will Include
said Rices house & So to Extend Westward - - - - as far as Said
Rices land goes -- -- and northward as far as ye prison yard now is

Solomon Johnson of Leicester In the County of Worcester Gent.
being Convicted of Drunkenness by the View of the Justices in
Court, & it being a second Conviction—The Court thereupon order & Sentence him that he pay a fine of Ten Shillings to the use
of the Poor of the Town of Worcester where the offence was Comitted or Stand Comitted in his majestys Goal in Worcester by the
Space of Twenty four Hours & pay Cost & Fees and Give bond
by way of Recognizance with Suretys for the Good behaviour till
the Court of Generall Sessions of the peace to be held here in November next vizt The said Solomon Johnson in Ten pounds & the
Suretys in five pound Each and to stand Comitted till Sentence is
performed & he failing of So doing The Court ordered The Clerk
To Issue out a mittemus accordingly which was done

The Court now order that a Sutable Vault for Receiving the
ordure of those who are or may be Confined in the Goal in Worcester be made as Soon as may be & that due Care be had in
making the Same Strong and well plateing the hole to be Cut
through the floor into the Same & making of it very secure and
William Jenison and Daniell Gookin Esqr are appointed To See
the Same Effected at the Charge of the County

The Select men of Lunenburg presented a warrant directed to
their Constable to warn Ebenezer Slinglee & his family to depart
their Town and being duly Served was approved

The Select men of Dudley presented a warr' directed to their Constable to warn Martha Mackintire to depart their Town &ct which was approved it being Duly Served

---

The Selectmen of Mendon presented a Warr' directed to their Constable to warn Mary Wilson to depart their Town &ct which being duly Served was approved—also another To warn Benjⁿ Ramsdell & his wife to depart their Town approved in like maner

---

The Select men of Shrewsbury presented a warrant directed to their Constable to warn Thomas Foster to depart their Town which being duly Served was approved

---

A By law of the Town of Mendon Respecting Rams was presented for allowance & Disapproved

---

Ebenezer Hows Recognizance Discharged

John Dakin of Lancaster in yᵉ County of Worcester husbandman being presented by the Grandjurors &ct for not attinding yᵉ Publick Worship of God &ct appeared & made his Excuse & was dismiss'd paying Cost

---

A Vote or By law of the Town of Brookfield Relateing To Rams approved of by the Court

---

Jonathan Harwood of Sutton in yᵉ County of Worcester husbandman appeared in Court To answer To his presentment for not attending on yᵉ Publick Worship of God, and made his Excuse & was Dismiss'd paying Costs

Martha Mackintire of Dudley or Resident in Dudley Single woman Stood bound over To this Court by way of Recognizance by John Chandler Esqr To answer for the Crime of fornication appeared in Court & Confess'd ye Crime was find To the King thirty Shilling & Cost which She paid.

———

Ruth Ballard of Lancaster &c̃t being bound over to this Court In aug : 1735 by Mr Justice Wilder To answer for ye Crime of fornication her Recognizance was Continued To this Court & She now appeared & Confess'd her Self Guilty was find thirty Shillings To ye King & Cost wch She paid

———

Sam^{ll} Davenports Recognizances Discharged

———

Nathan Dennis of Dudley in the County of Worcester husbandman being bound over To this Court by way of Recognizance, By John Chandler Esqr To answer To a Complaint made against him by Martha Mackintire of Said Dudley or Resident in Said Dudley Singlewoman for his being the father of a Bastard Child begotten of her body, &c̃t appeared in Court, but made no Defence, To the Charge made against [him] Whereupon the Court ordered that the Said Nathan Dennis Enter into Recognizance with Suretys To Save ye Town of Dudley from any Charge on acco^t of Said Bastard Child vizt ye Said Nathan Dennis in the Sum of one hundred pounds & his Suretys in fifty pound Each which he then Did & John Rich of Dudley aforesaid & William Wait of Sutton In said County were his Suretys, and is as follows, personally appeared the said Nathan Dennis John Rich and Wm Wait and acknowledged themselves Indebted To Jonathan Hobbs of Dudley aforesaid husbandman & Treasurer of Said Town of Dudley and to his Successors for ye use of Said Town of Dudley in the Respective Sums following vizt the Said Nathan Dennis Principall in the Sum of one hundred pound and the Said John Rich and William Wait Suretys in the Sum of fifty pounds Each To be Leveyed upon their goods and Chattells Lands or Tenaments & for want thereof upon their bodys for the Use of ye Said Jonathan Hobbs present Town Treasurer of Said Dudley and of his Successors in said office for the use of Said Town if Default be made in the performance of ye Conditions here under written The Condition of this Recognizance is such That if the said Nathan Dennis Shall & doo well & Truely save and Indemnifie said Town of Dudley from any Charge Legally laid upon them On acco^t of Said Bastard Child Then the Recognizance to be void Else to abide in full force & Virtue Recognized before ye Court Att^s John Chandler J^r Cler

---

A Petition of Isaac Tomlin, of Westborough in ye County of Worcester Yeoman one of the Children of Ruhamah Wait late of Southborough Dec^d Seting forth that some time since ye Court were pleased To order how the said Ruhamah should be maintain'd by her Children &c^t Dureing her natural life but no provision was made respecting her funerall Charges praying the Courts Direction herein Read and The Court order That the funerall Charges of the said Ruhamah Wait being Three pound Seven Shillings Together with the Cost of prefering this petition be paid by the Children and Grand Children of ye Said Dec^d in the Same proportion as her maintainance was ordered by this Court in August 1735

A Petition of Daniel Mackintire and Sundry others Inhabitants of the Town of Oxford Seting forth the Great Difficulty they labour under for want of a Sutable and proper Road from their Dwellings to Travell in on Lords days To ye Publick worship of God in Said Town as well as on other days on their own business and that altho' they have applyed To ye Select men of oxford cant as yet obtain the same praying for Reliefe according to law which Petition was accompanyed with a Petition from the Selectmen of said Town of Oxford Showing to this Court That Sundry of the Inhabitants and proprietors of said Town have of late made application to them for private and Town ways which The petitioners apprehend ought to have Refference to Country and County highways with Respect to Causeways & Bridges, &ct praying the Court to Interpose in ye affair and that proper highways in said Town may be ascertained, which Petitions were Read, and the Court order That William Jenison & Henry Lee Esq^rs and Capt Benjamin Flagg or any two of them be a Comittee to Repair to oxford and to view & Consider what highways are of necessity to be laid out, in said Town, and also what may be proper for the Court to doe with Respect To ye Petition of Dan^ll mackintire and others, and make Report as soon as may be and the Petitions are Refered in the mean time for further Consideration

Joss Wheeler Son of Benjamin Wheler of Lancaster In ye County of Worcester husbandman being presented by ye Grand Jurors of Said County for droping and Covering Indian Corn on the ninth day of May 1736 at Lancaster aforesaid which day was ye Sabath or Lords day which action is Contrary to ye peace of our Lord ye King his Crown & Dignity & ye laws of this province in y^t behalf made & provided &ct. appeared in Court and Confessd him Self Guilty of Labouring but said he was Ignorant that therein he had broke ye laws of ye land, and being fully heard, Its Considered by ye Court that the Said Joss Wheeler pay as a fine for ye use of the Poor of ye Town of Lancaster the Sum of fifteen Shillings that he pay Costs & fees & Stand Comitted Till Sentence is performed.

he paid ye fine & Cost in Court

Hanah Wheeler wife of Benjamin Wheeler of Lancaster in ye County of Worcester husbandman being presented by ye Grand Jurors of Said County for droping or planting Indian Corn on the ninth day of May 1736. at Lancaster aforesaid which ninth day of May was ye Sabath or Lords day which action is Contrary to ye peace of the King &ct as p̃ ye presentment appears—appeared in Court and Confess'd herself Guilty of Labouring but said she was Ignorant that therein she had broke ye laws of ye land and being fully heard, Its Considered by ye Court that ye said Hanah Wheeler pay as a fine for ye use of ye Poor of ye Town of Lancaster the Sum of fifteen Shillings that she pay Cost & Fees and Stand Comitted till Sentence is performed : She paid ye fine & Cost in Court.

Benjamin Wheeler of Lancaster In ye County of Worcester Husbandman being presented by the Grandjurors of Said County for droping Corn and Covering it on ye ninth day of May 1736 at Lancaster aforesaid which day was ye Sabath or Lords day Contrary to ye peace of ye King &c^t as P ye presentment appears. he appeared in Court and Confess'd himself to be Guilty of Labouring but said It was Ignorantly done & not with intent to Break ye laws of ye land, and being fully hear[d] Its Considered by ye Court that the Said Benjamin Wheeler pay as a fine to ye use of ye Poor of ye Town of Lancaster The Sum of fifteen shillings that he pay Cost & fees & Stand Comitted till ye Sentence is performed He paid ye fine & Cost in Court

---

Rachell Newton ye wife of Abraham Newton of Southborough in ye County of Worcester Husbandman being presented by ye Grandjurors for said County at ye Court of Generall Sessions of the Peace held at Worcester within and for the County of Worcester on the first Tuesday of feb^{ry} last past for not attending ye Publick Worship of God for more yⁿ one Month preceeding the presentment and The Said Abraham Newton Recognizeing to his Majestye before William Ward Esqr one of his Majestys Justices of ye peace for Said County in five pounds for the Said Rachells appearing at this Court and to do and Receive that which by the Court shall be then & there enjoyned her & not to depart without Lycence, The said Rachell now appeared and made her Excuse and being fully heard Its Considered by the Court that the Said Rachell Newton Pay Cost Taxed at
and then be Dismissed, but She failing of so doing, and Departing without the Lycence of ye Court, and the said Abraham Newton failing of appearing and paying the Same altho' he was three times Solemnly Called upon to bring her into Court his Recognizance

was by the Court declared forfeited and the Clerk ordered to put the Same in Suit accordingly after which Said Abraham appeared and moved To have ye affair Reconsidered &c̄t was & further Refered To november next

———

A List of Inholders and Retailors Lycenced by this Court with ye Names of their Suretys Each principall Recognized in fifty pound and Each Surety in Twenty five pounds

The following persons are Inholders unless Retailor is added to there names

Worcester {
Capt Daniell Heywood   Suretys Capt Moses Rice Capt Benja Flagg
Capt Moses Rice Suretys Capt Benja Flagg & John Harwood
Mr Tho Starns Suretys Capt Flagg & Henry Lee Esqr
Mr John Bigelo Suretys Isaac Farnsworth Robt Horn
Mr John Crosby Retailor Suretys Danl Hubbard Jona Sargent
}

Lancaster {
Capt Thomas Carter Suretys Samll Willard Esq Capt William Richardson
Capt William Richardson Suretys Saml Willard Esq Capt Tho Carter
Mr Jonathan Houghton Jr Suretys Saml Willard & Edward Hartwell Esqr
Mr Benja Houghton Suretys Eleazer Heywood & John Sadler
Samuell Willard Esqr Retailor Suretys Capt Tho Carter & Capt William Richardson
}

Mendon {
Mr Ebenr Merriam
Capt William Rawson   bound for one another
Capt Daniel Lovett
}

Woodstock {
Capt Jonathan Payson Suretys Joseph Lyon & Eleazer Heywood
Mr Joseph Wright Suretys Capt Jona Payson & Capt Benja Flagg
}

Brookfield {
Mr Eleazer Heywood Surety Daniell Gookin Esqr Capt
Mr Solomon Keyes   [Jno Hubbard
Mr Nathaniell Read Suretys Capt James Leland Capt Joseph Willard
Capt Phillip Goss Capt Moses Rice principall Suretys Capt Flagg Jno Harwood
Mr Israel Richardson Suretys Jonathan Sargent Israell Richardson
}

Shrewsbury
{ Capt Daniell How   Suretys Caleb Witherbee John Crosby
  Mr John Bush Suretys Nahum Ward Esqr Capt Benja Flagg
  Nahum Ward Esqr } Retailors   Suretys Capt Benja Flagg
  Mr John Crosby   }   [Jno Harwood
  Suretys Peter Smith Danll Hubbard

Sutton
{ Mr Perez Rice   Saml Dudley Esqr principall Suretys Edwd
                         Hartwell Esqr Benja Flag
  Mr Obadiah Walker } Suretys for each other & Samll Read
  Mr Joseph Boyden }   for both
  Mr Eleazer Fletcher   Suretys Nathll Sherman Samuel
                                  Wadkins

Rutland
{ Capt Hubbard   Moses How principall } Nehemiah How &
  Mr Moses How Retailor   } Eleazer Heywood
                                 Suretys for both

Leicester
{ Mr Jonathan Sargent Suretys Eleazer Robins Ephraim
                                Witherbee
  Mr Thomas Richardson Suretys David Fay Isaac Farnsworth
  Mr James Smith Suretys Israel Richardson Jona Sargent
  Mr Wm Larkin Retailor Suretys Nahum Ward Esqr Nathan
                                 Carpenter

Southborough
{ Mr Robert Horn   Suretys John Crosby & Joseph Crosby
  Mr Caleb Witherbee Suretys John Croseby & Joseph Crosby

Uxbridge
{ Mr Samuell Read   Suretys Joe Boyden Obediah Walker
  Mr Ezekiell Wood   Surety Danll Hubbard Perez Rice
  Mr Solomon Wood principall Samll Read Suretys Joseph
                         Boyden Obedia Walker
  Mr John Harwood Retailor Suretys Capt Flagg & Joseph
                                    Dyer

Westborough
{ Capt John Fay   Suretys Saml Willard and Edward Hart-
                             well Esqrs
  John Maynard   Suretys Saml Willard and Edwd Hartwell
                                Esqrs
  Barzaleel Eager Retailor   Suretys Nahum Ward and Henry
                                 Lee Esqrs

Harvard
{ Mr Eleazer Robins Suretys Jonathan Sargent Ephraim
                             Witherbee
  Mr Eb: Sprague Suretys Benja Houghton James How

Lunenburg
{ Mr Ephraim Witherbee Suretys Saml Dudley Edward
                         Hartwell Esqrs
  Mr Isaac Farnsworth   Suretys John Biglo Robert Horn
  Josiah Willard Esqr Retailor Suretys Caleb Witherbee &
                                  Saml Dudley Esqr

Oxford
{ Mr Elijah Moore   Capt Moore principall Suretys Danl
                             Newhall Joe: Crosby
  Capt Moses Marcy   Capt Flagg principall Suretys Jno
                          Harwood Joseph Dyer

21

Dudley | Mr Daniel Coburn Suretys Isaac Barnard Moses How

Grafton
{ Capt James Leland Suretys Capt Joseph Willard Nath Read
Mr Nehemiah How Suretys Moses How Eleazer Heywood
Capt Joe Willard Suretys James Leland Nathll Read
Mr Nathll Sherman Suretys Isaac Barnard Ele: Fletcher

Upton
{ Mr John Sadler Suretys Benja Houghton Ephraim Hill
Mr John Hazeltine Jno Hazeltine principall Suretys Capt
Flagg & Jos: Dyer
Mr Saml Watkins Retailor Suretys John Sadler Ephraim
Hill

New
Sherborn
{ Mr Ephraim Hill Suretys John Sadler Ephraim Hill
Mr William Stockwell

New Medfield | Mr John Stacy Capt Flagg principal Suretys Jno Harwood
& Joseph Dyer

Lambs Town | Mr Nathan Carpenter Suretys Joseph Dwight Esqr William
Larkin

At one of ye Narragansett Towns | Fairbank Moore Suretys Joseph Dwight
Samll Willard Esqrs

William Jenison Esqr from ye Comittee appointed by this Court in May last on a Petition of Sundry persons to view and make Report of ye necessaty of laying out a Publick Road from the Town of Worcester To Sutton, made Report which was accepted and the Court order that the Clerk Grant out a warrant Directed to the Sheriff, To Impanell a Jury agreeable to law for ye laying out Said Road—to assemble at ye Dwelling House of Mr Joseph Boyden in Sutton on Tuesday the first day of October next to be duly Sworn for that end and that in laying out said Road they have due Regard to the Report of the Comittee

WORCESTER SS *Anno Regni Regis Georgi Secundi*
nunc Magnæ Britaniæ Franciæ et Hiberniæ
Decimo◯

Att a Court of Generall Sessions of the Peace begun and Held at Worcester In and for the
County of Worcester on the first Tuesday of
November being the Second day of Said Month
anno Domⁿ 1736

JUSTICES PRESENT

John Chandler   Esqrs   Henry Lee Esqr
Joseph Wilder   ⎱ Justices of   Nahum Ward Esqr
William Ward   ⎰ the Peace   John Keyes Esqr
William Jenison   ⎱ and Quo-   Justices of the Peace
John Chandler J^r   rum

———

Capt James Wilder   Mr Seth Chapin Junr   Mr Joseph Wright
Mr Gershom Rice Coroners

———

Grandjury

Mr Robert Goddard foreman

Mr David Fay   Mr John Daly
Mr Thomas Rice   Mr John Ayres   Mr James Whiple
Mr Cyprian Stevens   Mr Nath^{ll} Green
Mr Elias Sawyer   Mr Joseph Taft   Each attended Two days
Mr Nathan Tyler   Mr Sam^{ll} Davis   and Richard Wild Dept
Mr Joseph Lyon   Mr Symon Maynard Sheriff attended them

An acco[t] of Daniel Gookin Esq[r] Sheriff of the County amounting To Twenty one pound four Shillings Read and allowed and ordered that the Sum of Twenty one pound four Shillings be paid out of the County Treasury to Said M[r] Sheriff Gookin in full discharge thereof

---

James orcutt bound over to this Court by the Hon[ll] John Chandler Esq[r] To answer to his presentment by y[e] Grandjurors for the Crime of fornication appeared and was dismiss'd paying Cost

---

The Court now order that a Tax or assessment amounting to the Sum of Two hundred pounds be Raised on the Severall Towns within this County for defraying the usual & necessary Charges ariseing within the Same and that the Clark forthwith send out Warrants directed to the Selectmen or assessors of the Respective Towns within the County for assessing their Severall parts & proportions according to the Rules for assessing the last Province Tax and for paying the Same to Capt Benjamin Flagg County Treasurer or to his Successor at or before the last day of May next.

The Severall Towns Proportion thereof is as follows viz[t]

Worcester Twelve pound Eighteen Shillings & three pence	12	18	3
Lancaster Twenty nine pound Six Shillings & three pence	29	6	3
Mendon Nineteen pound Six Shillings & Ten pence	19	6	10
Woodstock Twenty pound four Shillings	20	4	
Brookfield Sixteen pound Eight Shillings & Eight pence	16	8	8
Southborough Elevin pound five Shillings & nine pence	11	5	9
Leicester Nine pound Twelve Shillings & five pence	9	12	5
Rutland Six pound one Shilling & five pence	6	1	5
Lunenburg Six pound Eight Shillings & Eight pence	6	8	8
Westborough Eleven pound Seven Shillings & Six pence	11	7	6
Shrewsbury Eleven pound four Shillings & five pence	11	4	5
Oxford Six pound Eighteen Shillings & five pence	6	18	5
Sutton thirteen pound Sixteen Shillings & Seven pence	13	16	7
Uxbridge Nine pound Nineteen Shillings & Eleven pence	9	19	11
Harvard Eight pound & three pence	8	0	3
Grafton Seven pound & Eight pence	7	0	8

Sum Totall   £200   0   0

Warrants were Issued out November 15th 1736

att[s]   Jn[o] Chandler J[r] Clr

Upon a Motion made & Seconded The Court order that Daniel Gookin Esq[r] Sheriff of this County do at y[e] Court of Generall Sessions of the Peace to be held here in Febry next Give Surety unto y[e] Kings majesty for y[e] Due & faithfull discharge and performance of His office in all the parts thereof with two Sufficient Suretys himself in one Thousand Pound lawful money and his Suretys in Five Hundred pound Each and directed that the Clerk notifye him of this order that So he Comply Therewith agreeable to y[e] province Law in Page 120

And the Justices of Said Court being apprehensive it may be of Dangerous Consequence for y[e] Keye of the Prison to be Kept at any place from y[e] Same desire M[r] Sheriff Gookin to have y[e] [key] Kept by y[e] the Resident Keeper of Said Prison that So if any accident by fire should hapen the Prisoners might not Perish by fire

---

The Court order that the Sum of fourteen pound one Shilling be paid out of the County Treasury To M[r] Gershom Rice Jun[r] to Reimburse him the mony he has advanced for Labour in building a bridge over a River Called french River between Worcester and Oxford not in y[e] Bounds of any Town Twenty Shillings thereof to be paid To Capt Benjamin Flagg for his Trouble & Service as one of the Comittee The Residue To be in full for his own Service & mony advanced as aforesaid Said Bridge being built by order of Court

---

Abigail Richardson Recognized for her appearance at this Court To answer for presentment by y[e] Grandjurors for Seling Strong Liquor &c appeared & was Dismiss'd paying Cost

---

The Select men of The Town of Shrewsbury presented a Warrant directed to their Constable to warn Eleazer Harthan & his wife to depart their Town and y[e] Same being duly Served was approved by y[e] Court

The Select men of Worcester presented a Warr[t] directed to one of their Constables to warn James Hawes and Han[a] Hooker to depart their Town w[ch] being duly Served is approved

———

Skipper Fairfield of Sutton &ct Husbandman Recognized before M[r] Justice Jenison To appear at this Court &ct appeared and was Discharged

———

William Chapman and Ann his wife both of Woodstock appeared before Court pursuant To their Recognizance Given To the Hon[ll] John Chandler Esq[r] To answer for their being Guilty of y[e] Crime of Fornication were find 30/ Each & to pay Cost w[ch] They paid

———

Nathan Ainsworth and Hulda his wife both of Woodstock Stand bound over To this Court by the Hon[ll] John Chandler Esq[r] To answer To their being Guilty of the Crime of Fornication appeared were find Thirty Shillings Each & Cost w[ch] they paid

———

Abraham Newton of Southborough in y[e] County of Worcester husbandman having recognized to our Sovereign Lord the King In y[e] Sum of five pound before William Ward Esq[r] one of his maj[tys] Justices of y[e] peace for the County aforesaid that his wife Rachell now should appear at the Court of Generall Sessions of the peace held here in August last. which was Continued over To this Court To answer to her presentment for not attending y[e] Publick Worship of God &ct & y[e] Said Rachell not appearing altho' Solomnly Called to come into Court but made default and the Said Abraham Newton was Solomnly Called to Bring her into Court and did not appear but made default   The Court therefore declare y[e] Recognizance forfeited and that a writt of Scire facias be Taken out against the said Abraham Newton for y[e] Sum of five pounds and also for y[e] Costs and Charges occasioned by the non appearance of y[e] Said Rachell Newton

Abraham Newton of Southborough In ye County of Worcester husbandman having Recognized To our Sovereign Lord the King In ye Sum of five pounds before William Ward Esqr one of his Majestys Justices of the Peace for the County aforesaid that his Daughter Sybella Newton should appear at the Court of Generall Sessions of the peace held here in febry 1735/6 To answer to her presentment by ye Grandjurors for not attending on ye Publick Worship of God &ct and the Said Recognizance has been Continued to this Court and the Said Sybella altho' Solemnly Called to come into Court did not appear but made Default and the Said Abraham Newton tho' Solemnly Called to bring the Said Rachell into Court did not appear but made Default also the Court then declare the Said Recognizance to be forfeited and that a writt of Scire facias be Taken out against the said Abraham Newton for the Sum of five pounds and also for the Cost and Charges Occasioned by ye non appearance of ye Said Sybella Newton

———

Daniell Gookin Esqr Sheriff made Return of the Warrant Directed to him by order of the Court of Generall Sessions of the Peace in August last for the laying out of a Road from Worcester to Sutton under his own hand and Seal as also under the hands and Seals of The Jury by him impanelled which was accepted of by this Court and the Road Laid out & described therein is by the Court fully Established and the Warrant & ye proceedings thereupon are ordered to be Recorded, and is as follows

Worcester ss To the Sheriff of the County of Worcester or his Deputy Greeting Whereas ye Comittee appointed by ye Court of Generall Sessions of ye peace in may Last past have made Report Concerning a Publick Highway or Country Road between ye Towns of Worcester and Sutton being necessary to be Laid out as ⅌ ye Report on file appears. These are therefore in his maj-
[SEAL] esties Name to Require and Comand You or one of you to Sumon and Impanell a Jury of good and Lawful men Qualified according to Law to meet & assemble att ye Dwelling House of Mr Joseph Boyden in Sutton aforesaid Inholder on Fryday

yᵉ first Day of October next which Jury So Sumoned and Impanelled you are to Cause a proper oath to be administered to them
by a Justice of yᵉ peace for yᵉ County aforesᵈ and then to proceed
to view and Lay out a Publick Highway or Country Road between
yᵉ Towns aforesaid Pursuant to yᵉ Laws of this province & haveing
a Due Regard to yᵉ Report of yᵉ Late Comittee hereof fail not and
make Due Return hereof with your Doings herein to this Court att
their next Sessions of yᵉ peace to be held here on yᵉ first Tuesday
of Novemʳ. next as well under your own hand as yᵉ hands of yᵉ
Jury aforesaid Dated att Worcester this twenty eighth Day of September in yᵉ tenth Year of his majesties Reign anno Dom 1736

By Order of Court————John Chandler Jʳ Clerk paˢ

Worcester ss   October 1. 1736   By virtue of yᵉ within Written
Warrant I have Impanelled a Jury of twelve good and Lawful men
and had them Sworn as yᵉ Laws Direct who met att Sutton and
then Laid out a Country Road from Sutton to Worcester meeting
House as ℗ yᵉ Jurys Report herewith all adjoyned will appear
                                                    Daniel Gookin Sh

Worcester ss   October yᵉ 1 : 1736   then yᵉ Jury that was appointed by Daniel Gookin Esqʳ Sheriff of said County to Lay out
a way from Sutton to Worcester according to yᵉ writtin Warrant
personally appeared and was Sworn to act Imparcially and In Dif-
ferently to Lay out Said way and in Laying of it out to have a Regard to yᵉ Conveinance of yᵉ Publick as well as to particularly
parsons Interest and to have a Regard to yᵉ Courts order in Laying yᵉ Same   Sworn before me William Jenison Just of peace

Worcester ss :   October 2ᵈ. 1736   we whose names which have
hereunto Subscribed being Sumoned & impannelled by Daniel
Gookin Esqʳ. Sheriff of Said County for to Lay out a Country Road
of a Sufficient Wedth from yᵉ town of Sutton to yᵉ Town of Worcester according to yᵉ Direction of yᵉ Warrant herewith annexed
being Sworn before Wᵐ Jenison Esqʳ one of his majesties Justices
for yᵉ County of Worcester have viewed yᵉ premises and have Laid
out Said Road as followeth (vizᵗ) begining att yᵉ End of yᵉ Lane
[   ] the meeting House in Sutton & so by marked trees and
heaps of Stones in yᵉ Westerly Side of Said Road as formerly Laid

out by yᵉ Select men of Sutton by yᵉ house of Ebe : Daggit—Samuel Lilly John Singletary John Brown Robert Goddard and yᵉ Dwelling House which James Hulnow Dwellsin and to Sutton Line So by marked trees on yᵉ Westerly Side of Said Road to Worcester Line said Road to be three Rods wide through Sutton and to Worcester Line Excepting through yᵉ Land of Philip Chase two Rod and half by marked trees to yᵉ Said Chases Barn So to Run between Said Chases House and Barn by marks on yᵉ Southerly Side of yᵉ Crick to a Small tree marked near yᵉ Old Bridge over Said Crick thence to Run on yᵉ Easterly Side of a white oak tree marked on yᵉ west Side of yᵉ Road to yᵉ River thence over yᵉ River to a marked tree on yᵉ west Side of Said Road and So as yᵉ Select men of Worcester hath Laid out a Town Road and as yᵉ Road is now trod to yᵉ meeting House in Worcester Said Road from yᵉ River to Worcester meeting House to be as yᵉ Select men have Laid out formerly   Said Road was Laid out through Phillip Chases Land by Consent of Said Chase Who freely Gave yᵉ Land for Said Road through his farm   Dated at Worcester October yᵉ 2ᵈ. 1736   Gershom Rice and a Seal Samuel Dudley and a Seal Daniel Heywood and a Seal Benjᵃ. Flagg Junʳ. and a Seal John Stockwell and a Seal Perez Rice & a Seal Robert Goddard & a Seal John Stearnes & a Seal Thomas Stearnes and a Seal Jotham Rice and a Seal Jeremiah Bucknum and a Seal Daniel Ward & a Seal Daniel Gookin Sh & a Seal

Entered ℗ John Chandler Jʳ Cle pac

The account of yᵉ Charge of Viewing and laying out the aforesaid Road amounting to the Sum of Seventeen pound five Shillings allowed of by the Court and is Due to the following Persons vizt

	£	s	d
To the Comittee for viewing &ct Each 10/	1	10	0
To Daniell Gookin Esqr Sheriff fourty four Shillings	2	04	0
To yᵉ Justice for his Travell & Swearing the Jury	0	12	0
To the Jury Each 10/ If' day being on yᵉ Service Two days	12	0	0
To the Clerk for writings. Copys, Recording orders &ct thirty Shillings	1	10	0
	17	16	0

Ordered that the Charge of viewing and laying out the County Road from Worcester To Sutton amounting to the Sum of Seventeen pound fifteen Shillings be paid By the County The Town of Worcester and the Town of Sutton In the proportion following viz.ᵗ The County To pay fourty four Shillings & Six pence

2 4 6

The Town of Worcester The Sum of four pound

nine Shillings   4 9 0

and The Town of Sutton The Sum of Eleven pound

Two Shillings & Sixpence   11 2 6

―――――――

17 16 0

and that the Clerk Send To the Said Towns Copys of this order that So they may Respectively Assess the Respective Sums laid on them and pay the Same To the County Treasurer or his Successor at or before the Last day of May next Which Together with the Sum Which the County are to pay as abovesaid he is to pay to yᵉ persons to whom the Same is Respectively [due]

―――――――

Ordered that Phillip Chase His heirs or assignes have Liberty dureing the Pleasure of the Court to Keep Gates well hung a Cross the Country or County Road lately laid out a Cross his land in Two particular places provided he Suffer no other Incumbrance on the Same, & the Gates are Kept in proper order & Repair at all times to be opened as may be needed

―――――――

Solomon Johnson of Leicester In the County of Worcester Gent having on the Seventeenth day of August Last past Recognized before John Chandler Junʳ Esqʳ one of his majestys Justices of the Peace for the County of Worcester To our Sovereign Lord the King In the Sum of Ten pounds with Suretys viz.ᵗ Thomas Hopkins of Leicester Mason and Simon Gleeson of Oxford Labourer both in yᵉ County of Worcester Each in yᵉ Sum of five pounds Conditioned for yᵉ Said Solomon Johnsons appearance at this Court

To answer To Such matters & things as should be objected against him on his majestys behalf & to Continue & be of yᵉ Good behaviour towards his majestye and all his Leige people &ct as ᵖ yʳ Recognizance appears and the Said Solomon Johnson not appearing, altho' Solemnly Called to Come into Court, but made default and the Said Thomas Hopkins and Simon Gleeson The Suretys being also Solomnly Called to bring The Said Solomon Johnson into Court did not appear but made default The Court therefore order that the Said bond be forfeited and it was accordingly forfeited and ordered that a writt of Scire Facias be Issued out against yᵉ Said Thomas Hopkins and Simon Gleeson for yᵉ Sum of five pounds Each and also for yᵉ Costs & Charges occasioned by the non appearance of the Said Solomon Johnson

---

Obediah MacKintire of Oxford In yᵉ County of Worcester husbandman being presented for [not] attending yᵉ Publick Worship of God appeared and made his Excuse and was dismiss'd paying Cost

---

On a motion made ordered that the Clerk write to yᵉ Selectmen of Grafton a Copy of the order of this Court In May 1733. Relateing to yᵉ mony laid on them for their part of yᵉ Laying out yᵉ County Road from Mendon to Worcester that So they assess their Town & pay yᵉ Same to Wᵐ Jenison Esqr

WORCESTER ss *Anno R^1 R^s Georgij Secundi nunc Magnæ Britainiæ Franciæ et Hiberniæ &c Decimo*◯

Att a Court of Generall Sessions of the Peace begun and Held at Worcester within and for the County of Worcester by adjournment by order of y^r Great and General Court from the first Tuesday of February 1736/7 to the third Tuesday of Said month being the fourteenth day of Said month. and then Sett.

JUSTICES PRESENT

John Chandler   Esqrs   Henry Lee   } Esqrs Justices
Joseph Wilder   ⎫ Justices of   Nahum Ward } of the Peace
William Ward   ⎬ the Peace
William Jenison ⎭ and Quo-
John Chandler Junr   rum

———

Grandjury

Mr Robert Goddard foreman

	Mr John Ayres	Messrs Symon Maynard
Messrs Thomas Rice	Mr David Fay	Mr John Daly
Cyprian Stevens	Mr Nath^ll Green	Mr James Whiple
Elias Sawyer	Mr Joseph Taft	attended Two days Each
Nathan Tyler	Mr Samuel Davis	and Mr Wilds waited on
Joseph Lyon	Mr James Wright	them

Joseph Dyer of Worcester In the County of Worcester Gent appelant from a Sentence given against him by William Jenison Esqr one of His majestys Justices of the Peace for the said County upon the Complaint of Hannah Hooker of Worcester in said County Spinster on his majestys behalf as well as of her own Seting forth that the Said Joseph Dyer at Worcester aforesaid on or about ye month of October last past and since that time at Worcester aforesaid did wittingly and willingly make or Spread a lye or false Report of ye Complain^t by saying she ye Complain^t was with Child when he had no Just Grounds for his So doing all which action was with a designe to belye defame and abuse ye Complain^t &c^t as ꝑ the Warrant dated the Thirty first day of December last past appears and before ye Said Justice was convicted of Spreading a false Report of the Said Hannah Hooker by Saying that She was with Child as set forth in ye Warrant & thereupon Sentenced To pay a fine To the King &c^t of Ten shillings & to pay all Cost &c^t as ꝑ the Sentence of Said Justice appears. and now the appellant appeared and to the Said Complaint Pleaded not Guilty The Evidences in the Case being Sworn and the Case fully heard on both Sides was Committed to the Jury who were Sworn according to law to Trye ye Same and Return'd their Verdict therein upon Oath as follows vizt That the Said Joseph Dyer is Guilty of Spreading an evil Report of Hannah Hooker Its therefore Considered by the Court that the Said Joseph Dyer Pay as a fine to our Sovereign Lord the King for and toward the Support of the Government of this province and the Incident Charges thereof Ten Shillings and that he pay Cost & Fees Tax'd at Six pound fourteen Shillings & nine pence and upon his neglecting to pay the Same The Court order Execution To be awarded therefor and that it be paid into the hands of the Clerk to be by him paid To whom the same is due Ex: march: 14th: 1736/7, & ye fine & Costs paid into the Court by Mr Sheriff Gookins

––––––

Amariah Lyon late of Shrewsbury now of Poquiog[1] so Called in

––––––

[1] Now Athol.

yᵉ County of Worcester Husbandman appellant from a Judgment given against him by Samuell Wright Esqr &ct as ꝑ yᵉ Sentence appears. upon yᵉ Complaint of William Temple of Worcester &ct upon his majestys behalf as well as of his own The partys appeared and the Case fully Considered The Court order the whole proceedings to be Quash'd & Each party to pay his own Cost

Amariah Lyon late of Shrewsbury now of Poquiog So Called In yᵉ County of Worcester appelᵗ from a Judgment given against him by Samuell Wright Esqʳ upon the Complᵗ of William Temple of Worcester &ct as ꝑ yᵉ Complaᵗ & Sentence appears The partys appeared and the Case being fully Considered The Court order The whole proceeding to be Quash'd and Each party bear his Costs

Samuell Stow of Lunenburg in yᵉ County of Worcester Gent being presented by the Grandjurors of Said County for not attending the Publick Worship of God &ct appeared and made his Excuse & was dismiss'd & he is to pay Cost Tax'd at   and not to depart without Lycence of the Court.

The Town of Lunenburg being presented by yᵉ Grandjurors &ct for not being provided with a Schoolmaster agreeable to law &ct appeared by their Selectmen and were Dismiss'd pay Cost which were paid

The Town of Mendon being presented by yᵉ Grandjurors &ct for not being provided with a Gramer School master according to law appeared by their Selectmen and it appearing They were now provided they were *dismiss'd* paying Cost—pᵈ

Jacob Aldrich Sealer of Leather for mendon Sworn before the Court

The Town of Sutton being presented by y⁰ Grandjurors &ct for not being provided with a School master &ct appeared by their Selectmen & were Excused paying Cost pᵈ

Nathan MacKintire of Oxford in yᵉ County of Worcester being presented by the Grandjurors appeared and made his Excuse and was Dismiss'd paying Cost pᵈ

Naomi ffarr wife of Joseph ffarr of Southborough in yᵉ County of Worcester Husbandman being presented by the Grandjurors for not attending on yᵉ publick worship of God &ct. She not being able to Come to Court her husband appeared and it appearing that it is through Indisposition of body That has Rendered her Uncapable of attending She was Dismiss'd pay yᵉ officer & attorney their Fees

William Temple's Recognizance Discharged

The Selectmen of Worcester presented to the Court a warrant directed to one of their Constables To Notifi Henry Wisdom with his wife and Three Children to depart yᵉ Town &ct and it appearing to have been duly Served was approved by yᵉ Court

Worcesters, Leicesters, & Rutlands presentments Continued Till may next

Duncan mᶜfarland of Rutland in yᵉ County of Worcester husbandman before yᵉ Court behaveing himself in a Rude manner & especially towards Wᵐ Temple of Worcester In yᵉ County of Worcester husbandman the Court order yᵗ he Recognize with Two Suretys himself in Twenty pound and his Suretys in Ten pound

Each for his appearance at the Court of Generall Sessions of ye peace to be held at Worcester In and for ye County of Worcester In may next To answer To Such matters & things as shall be objećted against him on his majestys behalf and in ye mean time to be of ye Good behaviour towards his majesty and all his Leige people and Especially Towards ye Said Wm Temple and to doe and Receive that which by ye Said Court Shal be then & there enjoyned him, &ćt wch he did & Daniell Campbell of Rutland aforsy^d & Benjamin Bartlett of Brookfield in said County Husbandmen were his Suretys

---

William Temple of Worcester In ye County of Worcester husbandman before ye Court behaveing himself in a Rude maner and Especially towards Duncan m^{c}farland of Rutland in ye County of Worcester husbandman The Court order that he Recognize with Two Suretys himself in Twenty pound and his Surety Ten pounds Each for his appearance at the Court of Generall Sessions of ye peace to be held at Worcester In and for the County of Worcester in May next To answer to Such matters and things as Shall be objećted against him on his majestys behalf, and in the mean time to be of ye good behaviour towards his majestye & all his Leige people and Especially Towards ye Said Duncan m^{c}farland and to doe and Receive that which by Said Court shall be then and there enjoyned him &ćt which he did and Joseph Wooly housewright and Peter Jenison Taylor both of Worcester aforesaid were his Suretys

---

John Biglo of Worcester In ye County of Worcester Inholder being presented by the Grandjurors for ye County of Worcester for allowing Wm Temple of Worcester afores^d Husbandman to be at his house at an unseasonable time of ye night & there Suffering of ye Said Temple to abuse Duncan m^{c}farland &ćt appeared in Court and made his Excuse & was Dismiss'd paying Cost

The Selectmen of yᵉ Town of Worcester presented to yᵉ Court a Warrᵗ directed to one of their Constables to notifie & warn Henry Wisdom with himself & three Children to depart yᵉ Town &ᶜᵗ being duly Served is accordingly approved.

———

A Petition of Daniell Taylor John Amsden and John Snow agents for the Town of Southborough In the County of Worcester presented to yᵉ Court a petition Seting forth That Margarett Taylor wife of John Taylor late a Resident in yᵉ Town of Southborough & a little boy named Abraham Son of yᵉ Margarett being about Two years old are in poor and Indigent Circumstances (The Said John Taylor haveing gon away & left them) and Stand in need of Releife and are put upon the Town and also Shewing That Abraham Newton an Inhabitant of Said Southborough Father of yᵉ Said Margarett & Grandfather of yᵉ Said Abraham Son of yᵉ Said Margarett, is possess'd of a Considerable Estate notwithstanding which he does nothing towards yᵉ Relief of his Said Daughter & Grandson praying yᵉ Court To order proper Reliefe to be made by Said Abraham towards yᵉ Relief of yᵉ his Daughter &ᶜᵗ   Read and ordered that the Petitioners Serve The Said Abraham Newton with a Copy of this Petition that So he Shew Cause if any he have at the next Court of Generall Sessions of the Peace To be holden at Worcester in and for yᵉ County of Worcester on yᵉ Second Tuesday of may next why he Should not be assessed according to law for yᵉ Support and maintainance of his Said Daughter & Grandson

———

The Court order that The Sum of Seven Shillings be paid out of yᵉ County Treasury To Capt Daniel Heywood for Expences in apprehending Phillip Kenison a Criminall or Capitall offender

———

The Selectmen of yᵉ Town of Lunenburg presented to yᵉ Court a warrant directed to one of their Constables to warn Nathan Barron of Groton &ᶜᵗ with his wife and Three Small Children To leave their Town and it being duly Served was approved by yᵉ Court

23

WORCESTER ss *Anno R¹ Rˢ Georgij Secundi nunc Magnæ Britainiæ Franciæ et Hiberniæ Decimo*

Att a Court of Generall Sessions of the Peace begun and Held at Worcester in and for the County of Worcester on the Second Tuesday of May being the Tenth day of Said month anno Dom 1737   .

John Chandler
Joseph Wilder   ⎱ Justices of yᵉ
William Ward   ⎰ Peace and
William Jenison   ⎰ Quorum
John Chandler Junʳ

Daniel Taft
Joseph Dwight
Samuel Wright ⎱ Esqʳˢ Justices
Henry Lee   ⎰ of the
Nahum Ward   ⎰ Peace
Samˡ Willard
John Keyes

Old Grandjury

Mʳ Robert Goddard foreman

	Mʳ David Fay	Mʳ Benjᵃ Goodrich
Mʳ Thomas Rice	Mʳ Simon Maynard	Mʳ James Daly
Mʳ Cyprian Stevens	Mʳ Jonathan Ferbus	Mʳ James Whiple
Mʳ Elias Sawyer	Mʳ Nathˡˡ Green	Richard Wilds Depᵗ
Mʳ Nathan Tyler	Mʳ Samuel Davis	Sheriff attended on
Mʳ Joseph Lyon	Mʳ James Wright	them and Each per-
Mʳ John Ayres	Mʳ Joseph Taft Junʳ	son attended 3. days

Grandjury Return'd to Serve ye present Year

Southborough Capt Dan^{ll} Taylor foreman

Worcester Mr James Holdin
   Mr Tyrus Rice
Lancaster Mr Gamaliell Beman
Mendon Mr Josiah Adams

Woodstock Mr John May[ ]
Brookfield Mr John Rich

Westborough Mr Charles Rice

Shrewsbury Mr Sam^{ll} Crosby

Sutton Mr Elisha Putnam
Leicester Mr John Whittemore
  Mr Eleazer Ward Oxford
Rutland Mr Sam^{ll} Brown
Uxbridge Mr John Cook

Lunenburg Mr John Heywood
Harvard Mr Jonathan Sawyer

Grafton Mr Nehemiah How

were Sworn all those y^t have ye mark under their names viz —— & sent home after ye Charge was given

John Chandler Junr Esqr presented an acco^{tt} for buying three books amount to the Sum of fourteen pound fourteen shillings wch was allowed of by the Court and order that the Treasurer of ye County pay To ye accountant John Chandler Junr Esqr fourteen pound fourteen Shillings in full thereof

An acco^t of the Travell and attendance of the Grandjury from may 1736 To may 1737 amounting unto ye Sum of Eighty Eight pound fourteen Shillings being presented for allowance was Examined by ye Court and allowed and The Treasurer order To pay ye Same to whome it is Due

ordered that the Sum of Twenty Seven shillings be allowed and paid out of the County Treasury To William Jenison Esqr for diging a vault &c^t under the Goal

Capt Benjamin Flagg County Treasurer presented his acco^tt from may 1736 To may 1737 which was Carefully Examined in Court whereby it appears he has made payments amounting To ye Sum of one hundred Sixty two pounds & three pence of which he is discharged & ye ballance of his acco^tt being ninety one pound fourteen Shillings & Seven pence he is Still to acco^tt for when Rec^d and the Court direct the Clerk to Sign his acco^t in their name

---

Benony Boynton of Lunenburg in ye County of Worcester husbandman having on the Tenth day of September last past Recognized before Josiah Willard Esqr one of his Majestys Justices of ye peace for ye County of Worcester to our Sovereign Lord the King In the Sum of five pounds lawfull mony of New England with Suretys vizt Benjamin Bellows of ye Town & County aforesaid husbandman and Samuell Davice of ye Town & County aforesaid Carpenter in ye Sum of fifty Shillings of ye Like mony Each Conditioned that the Said Benony Boynton Should personally appear before ye Court of Generall Sessions of ye peace held here in November last (which Recognizance was Continued from Court to Court till this time) to prosecute to Effect an appeal by him made from a Judgment Recovered against the Said Benony Boynton by John Grout on behalf of our Sovereign Lord the King at a Tryall before the Said Justice on ye Day & year aforesaid for ye payment of Cost &c^t as ⅌ ye Recognizance appears and the Said Benony Boynton not appearing tho' Solomly Called to Come into Court but made Default and the Said Benjamin Bellows & Samuell Davice the Suretys being also Solomly Called to bring ye Said Benony Boynton into Court did not appear but made Default The Court therefore order that the Said Recognizance be declared forfieted and it was accordingly declared forfieted and ordered that a writt of Scire facias be issued out against the Said Benjamin Bellows & Samuell Davice for y^e Sum of fifty Shillings Each lawfull mony of New England for y^e use of our Lord the King & also for y^e Cost & Charges occasioned by y^e non appearance of y^e Sald Benony Boynton

Gedion Cumstock of Smithfield in y^e Government of Road Island being bound over To this Court by Mr Justice Taft as $\widehat{p}^1$ y^e Recognizance appears Came into Court To answer y^e Same & was Dismiss'd paying Cost

An Foster of Lunenburg appeared in Court to answer to her presentment for not attending on y^e Publick Worship of God &c & was Excused & Dismiss'd paying Cost

Oliver Bly and Mary his wife being bound over to this Court to answer to their being Guilty of the Crime of Fornication, appeared in Court & Confess'd themselves Guilty   The Court therefore order they pay a fine of thirty Shillings Each &c & Cost & fees which They paid & were dismiss'd

Dunkin M^{c}farlands Recognizance Discharged

Vallontine Butler of Shrewsbury in ye County of Worcester being presented by ye Grandjurors for Traveling &c̄t on ye Lords day appeared and made his Excuse & was dismiss'd paying Cost

William Linsey of Rutland in ye County of Worcester being presented by ye Grandjury for prophane Cursing and Swearing appeared in Court pleading Guilty was find Ten Shillings & Cost & fees   pa'd

John Hinds of Brookfield in ye County of worcester husbandman being presented by the Grandjurors for the Crime of Drunkeness pleaded Guilty & find Ten Shillings & paid Cost—In Two Cases

John Hinds of Brookfield in ye County of Worcester husbandman being presented by the Grandjurors for absenting himself from ye Publick Worship of God appeared in Court & made his Excuse & was Dismiss'd paying Cost

The Selectmen of Westborough presented to the Court a Warrant Directed to one of their Constables To Notifie & warn Doctor Joshua Wheat with his wife Elizabeth & four Children to depart y^t Town & it appearing to be duly Servd was approved

Josiah Wadkins of Upton in ye County of Worcester husbandman appellant from a Sentence or Judgment given agst him by Dan^{ll} Tafft Esqr &ct appeared in Court was find Ten Shillings & to pay Cost & fees wch he paid

The Select men of ye Town of Worcester presented to ye Court for approbation a Town Vote or Buy Law Relateing to Rams & was approved accordingly

Elizabeth Warner of Harvard In ye County of Worcester Single being bound over by Mr Justice Wilder To this Court to answer for her being Guilty of ye Crime of Fornication appeared Confess'd ye falt & was dismiss'd paying a fine of thirty Shillings & Cost

The Town of Leicester being presented for not being provided with a Schoolmaster according to law appeared and made an Excuse in behalf of the Town which being duly Considered they were Excused paying Cost

Thomas Ainsworth of Brookfield in ye County of Worcester husbandman appeared in Court to answer to his presentment by ye Grandjurors for Wilfully absenting himself from ye Publick Worship of God &ct and made his Excuse & was Dismiss'd paying Cost

Phillip Negro Servt To Samuell Dudley Esqr appeared in Court to answer To his presentment by ye Grandjurors his master being present who made his Excuse and he was dismiss'd paying Cost & fees

———

Nathaniell Dike Junr of Sutton in ye County of Worces[ter] husbandman appeared in Court To answer to Two presents against him for Wilfully absenting him Self from ye Publick Worship of of God &c^t & made his Excuse which was accepted & he was dismiss'd paying Cost

———

William Temples Recognizance Discharged

———

David Sanger of Woodstock In the County of Worcester husbandman appeared in Court To answer to his presentment by ye Grandjurors for absenting himself from ye Publick of God &c^t as appears ᵽ ye presentm^t he made Excuse & was Dismiss'd paying Cost

———

Peter Laurance of Grafton In the County of Worcester Indian planter appeared in Court To answer for his absenting himself from ye Publick Worship of God &c as ᵽ his presentment appears & made his Excuse which was accepted and he was Dismiss'd paying Cost

———

The Votes Sent in from ye Severall Towns for ye Choice of a County Treasurer and being opened in Court & Inspected it appeared that Capt Benjamin Flagg of Worcester was Elected by Every Vote and he was Sworn in Court to ye faithfull Discharge of his Office by ye Clerk ᵽ order of Court

———

Eleoner Kellog of Brookfield in ye County of Worcester Singlewoman being presented by the Grandjurors for our Lord ye King upon Oath for Comitting ye Crime of fornication at Brookfield

aforesaid having had a bastard Child there born of her body Sometime in yᵉ month of July 1736. Contrary to the peace of &ct as
also to the law in that Case made and provided as ꝑ yᵉ presentment made in augˢᵗ 1736 appears, and now the Said Eleoner Kellog being brought before yᵉ Court To answer for yᵉ Same, She
pleaded not Guilty & Thereupon The Court order that She pay as
a fine to our Sovereign Lord the King fifty Shillings or that She be
Severely Whip'd on the naked body, Ten Stripes on the Twelfth
Instant between yᵉ Hours of Three and four of the Clock afternoon
& that She pay Cost & Fees Taxed at five pound five Shillings &
Two pence & Stand Comitted till Sentence be performed & She
was Comitted to the Sheriff according with a Copy of the Sentence

---

Samuell Dudley Esqʳ of Sutton in yᵉ County of Worcester being
presented by yᵉ Grandjurors for Prophane Swearing appeared &
pleaded to yᵉ Insufficiency of yᵉ presentment wᶜʰ being duly Considered The Court order presentment to be Quash'd & yᵉ Sᵈ Dudley paid Costs

---

A memoriall of yᵉ Seleƈt men of Sutton Dated may 9ᵗʰ. 1737
praying yᵉ Court To alter yᵉ Country Road Lately laid out from
Sutton To Worcester vizᵗ part thereof near yᵉ present Dwelling
House of Phillip Chase &ct   Read and it is accordingly allow'd of
                    Attˢ   John Chandler Jun Cle pac

General Index.

General Index.

www.ingramcontent.com/pod-product-compliance
Lightning Source LLC
Chambersburg PA
CBHW030835270326
41928CB00007B/1055